Love, Oneness, and Radical Inclusion

Love, Oneness, and Radical Inclusion

The Legacy of Bishop John Shelby Spong

WILLIAM S. GEIMER

RESOURCE *Publications* · Eugene, Oregon

LOVE, ONENESS, AND RADICAL INCLUSION
The Legacy of Bishop John Shelby Spong

Copyright © 2025 William S. Geimer. All rights reserved. Except for brief quotations in critical publications or reviews, no part of this book may be reproduced in any manner without prior written permission from the publisher. Write: Permissions, Wipf and Stock Publishers, 199 W. 8th Ave., Suite 3, Eugene, OR 97401.

Resource Publications
An Imprint of Wipf and Stock Publishers
199 W. 8th Ave., Suite 3
Eugene, OR 97401

www.wipfandstock.com

PAPERBACK ISBN: 979-8-3852-4488-1
HARDCOVER ISBN: 979-8-3852-4489-8
EBOOK ISBN: 979-8-3852-4490-4

07/10/25

The Jerusalem Bible Doubleday & Company Inc. (1966)

Holy Bible (King James Version) Hendrickson Publishers Marketing LLC (2016)

Contents

Acknowledgments | vii
Introduction: A Buried Universal Guide to a Life of Love | ix

PART I | INTRODUCING THE FOURTH GOSPEL

Preface | 3
Chapter 1   Setting the Stage | 5
Chapter 2   John: One Gospel, More Than One Author | 10
Chapter 3   Separating John from the Other Gospels | 15
Chapter 4   The Work of a Palestinian Jew | 18
Chapter 5   Tracing the Jewish Roots of the Prologue | 20
Chapter 6   Permeating Wisdom: The Doorway to Jewish Mysticism | 23
Chapter 7   John the Non-Literalist | 26

PART II | THE BOOK OF SIGNS: MYTHOLOGICAL CHARACTERS WRAPPED INSIDE HISTORY

Chapter 8   The Mother of Jesus: Introduction to the Book of Signs | 33
Chapter 9   Nicodemus: What It Means to be Born of the Spirit | 36
Chapter 10   The Samaritan Woman at the Well: A New Dimension of the Jesus Experience | 40
Chapter 11   The Gentile Official's Son: The Meaning of God and Faith | 44
Chapter 12   The Man Crippled for Thirty-Eight Years | 48
Chapter 13   Andrew and Philip: The Red Sea and Manna | 54

CONTENTS

Chapter 14   The Brothers of Jesus: A Debate on Origins | 62
Chapter 15   The Man Born Blind: The Split from Judaism Is Complete | 67
Chapter 16   Lazarus: Breaking the Final Barrier | 72

PART III | THE FAREWELL DISCOURSES AND THE HIGH PRIESTLY PRAYER

Chapter 17   Peter and the Commandment to Love | 79
Chapter 18   Not Atonement but Glory! John Clarifies Jesus' Death | 82
Chapter 19   The Analogy of the Vine: God Is Indwelling, Not External | 93
Chapter 20   The Prayer of Jesus: Gethsemane Transformed | 96

PART IV | THE PASSION NARRATIVE: FROM DARKNESS TO LIGHT, FROM DEATH TO LIFE

Chapter 21   A Brief Introduction to the Climax of This Gospel | 101
Chapter 22   Judas: The Figure of Darkness | 103
Chapter 23   Peter: The Struggle Within the Soul | 107
Chapter 24   Pilate: The Conflict Between Survival and Truth | 112
Chapter 25   At the Cross: The Mother of Jesus and the Beloved Disciple | 117
Chapter 26   It Is Finished: Water and Blood Flow Together | 122

PART V | RESURRECTION: MYSTICAL ONENESS REVEALED

Chapter 27   Introducing John's Story of Easter | 129
Chapter 28   Magdalene: Do Not Cling to What Is, Journey into What Can Be | 133
Chapter 29   Peter and the Beloved Disciple: Resurrection Dawns Without a Body | 137
Chapter 30   Pentecost: The Second Coming of Jesus—It Was "A Little While" | 139
Chapter 31   Thomas: The Final Witness, the Ultimate Claim | 143
Chapter 32   The Epilogue: Resurrection Is Not Physical, but It Is Real | 146

Afterword | 149
Bibliography | 159

Acknowledgments

THE QUOTATIONS THAT BEGIN the book are taken from Bishop Spong's memoir *Here I Stand*. Thereafter, Spong quotations are from *The Fourth Gospel: Tales of a Jewish Mystic*. Quotations from Marcus Borg's *Reading the Bible for the First Time* are also included. Publication of all these works is by Harper Collins and is gratefully acknowledged.

Introduction

A Buried Universal Guide to a Life of Love

"I believe you are a prophet and I will strive with you to answer God's call to live fully, love wastefully, and be all that I can be. Thank you, thank you and may your life continue to be blessed."

"I hope the next plane on which you fly crashes. You are not worthy of life. If all else fails, I will try to rid the world of your evil presence permanently."

TODAY, UNFORTUNATELY, WE ARE not shocked at seeing such messages of adoration and vitriol directed to the same person. It was not always so. Even now, we might be surprised if we found that the person targeted was not a political figure; not a president or a candidate for that office; not a person of power at all. Indeed, just a member of the clergy. The recipient of the sentiments set out here was Episcopal Bishop John Shelby Spong.

While he was not what we would consider a power figure, Spong was known beyond the halls of Christendom. In the eighties and nineties, he appeared on popular national television shows, including *Oprah*. He counted as friends figures such as Desmond Tutu. His cousin was a US senator. Inside and outside the church, he did pioneering work on behalf of equality for women, gays and lesbians, and people of color well before those matters came to the forefront of national consciousness.

When he died in 2021 at the age of 90, Spong left a valuable gift. It is a gift to us all but a gift of particular value to some of us. It is a gift that

INTRODUCTION

has been consciously buried. The purpose of this book is to resurrect and re-present that gift.

The gift is a very different way to see the Jesus story. The gift is a very different way to envision what many call God, and our relationship with God. The gift is also the practical value of that different Jesus story in our lives today, not in the sweet by-and-by.

Spong described it this way: *The basis upon which Christianity can be reformulated so that its message can be heard in the echoes of the language of the twenty-first century and upon which we can build "A New Christianity for a New World."*

Those who may benefit most from the gift are the many of us who have been exposed to standard Christianity at some point in our lives but have abandoned it, often for very good reasons. Where then to go spiritually? "Nowhere" is the answer for many. That is especially true of those who, whether they would concede it in such stark terms, really consider themselves too intelligent for "religion." They go about their business with no apparent need to even consider that there is anything more, especially anything more that purports to have an enriching impact on their daily lives.

Unfortunately, the scions of organized religion have buried the gift. They have not done so out of fear or malice but because they are locked into their own security systems. They have patronizingly relegated the gift to the realm of scholarly theological discussion. But especially today, the gift is too important to remain interred in the crypt of polite academic exchange.

I am far from being any sort of expert, yet perhaps I am just the kind of person who is qualified to re-present the bishop's gift. I have traveled many spiritual paths, including standard Christianity, including standard Christianity in its evangelical form. Spong refers to us as "church alumni." I came to abandon standard Christianity. Folks like me are the majority in Western society, and our numbers are growing.

I have also had the benefit of advanced formal education. I know and respect the power of reason. Yet I am convinced that no one is sufficiently self-sufficient to ignore that which lies beyond reason.

So the question for us is this: If we are innately aware that there must be something more, but the Christianity to which we have been exposed no longer gives us any life value, then what? Following no spiritual path at all is certainly an answer, as is exploring other spiritual paths. I have done both.

But there is a lane on the Christian path that has been covered over. The Christianity that so many are quite content to do without is not at all

INTRODUCTION

like the gift of New Christianity. Spong's vision absolutely dismantles what most people think is Christianity. But from the ruins of an edifice created by an authoritarian male hierarchy centuries ago, New Christianity offers a positive vision that also shares much with other faith traditions around the world.

So my hope is that those described here will consider or reconsider a New Christianity, consider a radical new vision of the identity and purpose of the historical Jesus and its very powerful potential to enrich lives. Now. Today.

An important step in resurrecting this life-affirming, life-altering vision is setting it out in simpler, non-scholarly terms that might encourage former Christians and never-Christians to understand and consider it. To consider universal principles of love and oneness with God as a way of life. As you will see, that is not always easy. As a member of academia, I appreciate Spong's commitment to understandable writing. I believe he would have approved of my effort to simplify. He once observed that *Learned commentaries abound, but those for whom I write are not going to read them.* My field is law, and I have no doubt his statement applies to some of my work and that of my colleagues. In this book, however, perhaps my being neither theologian nor biblical scholar may give me an advantage and help me heed Spong's caution.

If people generally, and especially former Christians, are to be reached here and persuaded to consider how a New Christianity can enrich lives, my effort to present it cannot be overly scholarly or theological. Given the subject matter, that will be challenging. Nevertheless, I am committed to presenting an understandable outline of New Christianity. Be aware that in furtherance of that goal I employ several distinctly non-scholarly approaches.

First, rather than undertaking a scholarly "review of the literature," I rely primarily on only one source. It is Bishop Spong's take on John's gospel: *The Fourth Gospel: Tales of a Jewish Mystic*, written when he was 82.

To reveal the outline of New Christianity, I will examine each of the chapters in his book, in language that is as plain as I can make it.

I note that even in academic writing, a comprehensive survey of the literature on a subject cannot help but make that approach somewhat shallow, not to mention generally less readable. No one has the physical or intellectual capacity to examine every source in depth. Consequently, every scholarly inquiry is conducted at some level of superficiality. That is OK.

INTRODUCTION

Scholars are writing for a legitimate but very different audience and purpose than am I. For this work, I choose "deeper in fewer." I will occasionally refer to a few other sources. For references to the text of John's Gospel, I chose the Jerusalem Bible (1966). That is not to say, however, that readers will not benefit from examining the full exposition found in *The Fourth Gospel*. They will, and I recommend it, along with all of Spong's works.

As we journey through *The Fourth Gospel* chapter by chapter, we will see it reveal a new Jesus story, one that in all probability is quite different from the one you learned or heard about.

If we are to rely primarily on one source, we could not find a better one. By the time of his death, Bishop Spong was recognized as one of the world's most thorough religious scholars. His New Christianity is not simply an opinion piece. For our benefit, he has done the exhausting research, especially on the question of what was happening on the ground two thousand years ago, its context, and the perception some early Christians had of their experience with Jesus. That is another advantage of choosing to examine a book he wrote late in life. By the time the book appeared, he had read and thoughtfully considered every word ever written about the Gospel of John, as well as an incalculable number of writings about Christianity and organized religion generally. Admirably, he also alerts us to respected figures who disagree with him.

Second, part of my commitment to a non-scholarly approach means there will be no footnotes or endnotes. I highly recommend the works listed in the bibliography. I remain, however, willing to respond to any questions about sources and attribution.

Third, on the matter of attribution I will shamelessly quote, paraphrase, and summarize Bishop Spong, while staying true to his vision of the New Christianity as I understand it. Quotations of Spong will be in italics.

Fourth, I will include my own comments and interpretation. I do not find them to be at odds with what Spong is constructing. Quite the contrary. But the spiritual journey of each of us is unique, and I will occasionally see issues that I think Spong might have developed but for some reason did not.

Should you be moved to further inquiry by the story that will emerge here, know that Spong wrote many other books that explore his life-affirming approach. One in particular deserves special mention here. It is *Jesus for the Non-Religious*. Spong believed that the book represented a final resolution of the tension between his long-held view of Jesus as intensely human

INTRODUCTION

and profoundly Jewish, and the distortion of both by standard Christianity, including the church in which he held high office. With the greatest respect, I would disagree. I believe it all finally came together for him in his examination of John's Gospel. Much of the same vision is found in both books, but I believe *The Fourth Gospel* is the definitive work. I think that is particularly true because it contains more of an affirmative explanatory portrait of New Christianity to complement the deconstruction of standard teaching that he had developed in earlier works over the years. This book closes the circle.

A few additional observations that may help in understanding this new story. First, it is not a new story.

I am presenting nothing new here. The core elements of the New Christianity have long been recognized in theological circles. The Dominicans who compiled the Bible translation to which I refer acknowledged in the 1960s that John's Gospel recounts a Jesus story that differs significantly from that told in the other three.

There are even much earlier examples of insights on New Christianity. For example, Maximus, a sixth-century CE Byzantine monk, captured some of its essence. According to noted scholar Karen Armstrong, Maximus urged that if human beings emptied their minds of the jealousy and animosity that ruins their relations with one another, they could, even in this life, become divine. Our love of God was inseparable from our love of one another.

Unfortunately, the wisdom of Maximus, like that of the New Christianity, was buried. Imperial Christianity continued.

There are many other reminders that I am only re-presenting and representing something that has been around for quite awhile but has been tucked away by traditional church leaders and scholars.

We are of necessity drawing out the new story by examining stories from the Bible. That is the only place either story may be found. There is, of course, no "the Bible." There are almost as many Bibles as there are televangelists waving them at us today.

But any Bible we choose is necessarily the source for most of what we ordinary folks know about both standard Christianity and what we can learn about New Christianity. The importance of Bibles to Christianity presents both an obstacle and an opportunity. On one hand, there are so many legitimate concerns about the accuracy of the accounts in all of them that no reputable scholar would cite any of them as a reliable source on

INTRODUCTION

just about any subject. But Bibles are much more than fodder for scholarly debate. They offer us much that is of value to our daily lives, provided we learn to experience them in a different way.

The essence of a new way to look at the Bible is to be wary of literalism in respect of almost all of it. Are we reading about what really happened on the ground long ago? Or is some of what we are reading a product of the imagination or the agenda of the writers, editors, and revisers? Again and again, we will see that Spong cautions us against literalism. This means that again and again, the story of John is explained within the assumption that most of the words and actions attributed to Jesus and others simply did not happen on the ground. Accept that premise, and you have undermined a good deal of fundamentalist Christianity. What then could be left? A lot. A New Christianity. Beyond literalism there is much of value for us.

It is no accident that the New Christianity emerges most clearly from John's Gospel as opposed to the other three, known as the Synoptics. Origen, a Christian scholar who died about 1,800 years ago, recognized what the authors of John were doing differently. According to David Brakke, a contemporary scholar, Origen saw that a spirit inspired them to create a story that was historically false so that people would seek to understand the story's higher spiritual meaning.

I suspect that one of the reasons Spong in *The Fourth Gospel* cautions us so often against literalism is that he does not want us to be deprived of the rich life treasures that may be found simply by peeling away the layer of literalism. In these pages, we will reveal some of those treasures.

The perception of their experience with Jesus by what will be called the Johannine Christians some ninety years after his death has more for us than anything literal storytelling could offer. From their story emerges a Jesus with a different and more meaningful message for us than the one that orthodox Christianity of all types has been peddling for centuries.

New Christianity works in my life. And so, on his behalf, but with no endorsement or commission, I seek in this book to resurrect the New Christianity of John Spong. It has been pigeonholed and filed away as some sort of "liberal theology," reserved for learned discussion if noticed at all. It has definitely not been offered for consideration as part of the mainstream life of most churches. Such treatment does a disservice to the writers of those messages of both love and hate, and to many others. Especially today, there is great need for Spong's gift to be raised up and re-examined.

PART I

Introducing the Fourth Gospel

Preface

MUCH OF THIS SECTION is a standard biographical acknowledgment roll of those who influenced Spong's life and work. But there are parts that provide guidance for what is to come. An example:

> *I have arrived at a place both spiritually and theologically with which I am content... I resonate significantly with the retired bishop who once said to me, "The older I get the more deeply I believe, but the fewer religious beliefs I have." That, I think, is the mystical oneness to which all religious systems point and is thus the final goal of the religious journey.*

A spiritual learning journey never ends, but one hopes that there comes a point where anxiety and fear recede and we are satisfied that the key to our own path has been found.

The preface also lets us know that what will follow will be a radically new way of looking at Jesus:

> *I have discovered ... that if I walk the Christ path deeply enough and far enough, it will lead me beyond anything I now know about Christianity ... Jesus walked beyond the boundaries of his religion into a new vision of God ... God is ultimate. Christianity is not.*

I highlight this passage because it is the essence of Spong's contentions. He concludes:

> *I claim not that the Christian path is the exclusive path, but that it is the only path I know and thus the only path on which I can walk.*

PART I | INTRODUCING THE FOURTH GOSPEL

This statement was immensely important to me. I left the Christian path and learned much by traveling with other faith communities. Whether to return to a Christianity that was telling a story that I had come increasingly to disbelieve was difficult. Ultimately, like Spong, I came to realize that I must walk the only path I know.

A caution here. There is a great deal of introductory matter to get through if we are to appreciate both the unique nature of John's Gospel and the radical new Christian path it reveals. However, in the introductory chapters those new features gradually begin to appear. A new story is already being told. The conclusion of the book is as exciting as that found in a good thriller, and much more important. I urge you to be patient and consider the early chapters in that light. Spong is not just offering something different to see. He is offering a new way of seeing.

CHAPTER 1

Setting the Stage

Spong begins by recounting his initial negative reaction to the Gospel of John and his reasons for concluding that the common interpretation of it has been immeasurably harmful:

> *Because this book was thought to have spelled out "orthodox Christianity," John's gospel also helped to fuel such dreadful events in Christianity as heresy hunts and the Inquisition. As the centuries rolled by, John's gospel seemed to make meaningful discourse on the nature of the Christ figure almost impossible.*

I didn't like this Gospel either, because we both initially understood it this way:

> *John's Jesus claimed pre-existence—that is, he said he came to this earth from another life in another place.*

I wonder how many of us have never seriously considered the implications of this stunning claim, or its validity. For decades, I certainly did not. When I finally did, I found that I do not accept it any more than did Spong.

The reason most in the Christian tradition do not examine the claim probably lies with creeds, and the dogma built upon them. Spong traces this development, from the conversion of "Jesus is Messiah" in the Hebrew tradition, when Christians were mostly Jews, to "Jesus is Lord," when

PART I | INTRODUCING THE FOURTH GOSPEL

Greek culture took over and Christians were mostly gentiles. He traces this line to the development of the Nicene Creed in 325 CE and beyond. Today, millions of people in the Episcopal, Anglican, and Roman Catholic tradition still recite a version of this creed at least weekly.

Spong notes that *the creed attempted to define Jesus of Nazareth as the incarnation of a theistic God who lived in the sky and later as the second person of "the divine and eternal trinity."* He concludes that *creeds, by definition, are always barrier-building vehicles . . . creeds are ecclesiastical attempts to draw theological lines so firmly in the sand that it becomes easy to determine who is in and who is out.*

Creeds provided help in that sorting process, and the first issue was what to do with those who are "out." Early Christian officialdom answered this question the way all the orthodox religious hierarchies that followed do: persecute them. As Spong said further: *Imposed orthodoxy is never real and never vital. The creedal system seemed to me to have defined God as an invasive, miracle working deity from outer space, and to have made the work of engaging the world in dialogue not only very difficult, but almost impossible.*

Here we have the first contentions of Spong's New Christianity. Jesus did not, as God himself, come down from a "heaven" in human form. Creeds that are merely the products of the minds of humans three hundred years and more after his death are not true. Not only that: the kind of orthodoxy that produces creeds abets violence and injustice.

There is another aspect of imposed orthodoxy that Spong does not cover directly but which deserves a brief mention here. The danger for those who are "out" these days comes primarily from the religious right, known unfortunately as "evangelicals." A cruel equivalent of a creed motivates them to cast aside any uniting vision of the identity and teachings of Jesus in favor of raw power: power to impose their version of life on others and persecute them. The "outs" include all others, those from other spiritual paths or no path, who do not look or act as they do. It is impossible to determine how many of these followers of "power orthodoxy" are sincere and how many push it for more nefarious reasons. I will not try.

An illustrative piece of evidence, however, is an incident in December 2022. A Florida schoolteacher broke in on a group of Muslim students who were praying in the traditional prostrate position. She said, "I believe in Jesus, so I am interrupting the floor." She then stepped on their hands. One has to wonder where and how this woman's perception of Jesus was formed. The creed of power orthodoxy must be a prime suspect.

This is a particularly regrettable development given that the evangelical movement began in the US in the nineteenth century with campaigns against slavery, alcohol, oppression of women and other disadvantaged groups, and the mistreatment of prisoners. It has strayed far. Today there are reports of congregants complaining to pastors that they don't want to hear the beatitudes read at service, or anything about loving enemies. All those passages are deemed "weak."

In the opening chapter, Spong describes the process by which he came late in his career to see John's Gospel unfolding as the work of Jewish mysticism, and *the Jesus of John's Gospel suddenly became not a visitor from another realm but a person in whom a new God consciousness had emerged.* Note the choice of words. Jesus was a person, not a descending deity. He was a person in whom a new God consciousness emerged. He did not bring it with him.

Spong wanted readers to understand clearly the spiritual evolution that brought him to these conclusions. The process began with his increasing skepticism about "atonement theology," a focus on depravity and weakness that portrays God as a "divine rescuer." Atonement theology is an essential element of the standard Christian story, as well as the Jewish orthodoxy that Jesus challenged so fiercely. Spong's undertaking is to introduce us to a new vision. In it, "Jesus came to die for your sins" is not the real story. A sharing of the new God consciousness is.

Discovery of shortcomings and weaknesses in atonement theology brought Spong to consider not just how standard Christianity can be unhelpful and even dangerous; it also led him to construct what a new vision of the Christian story would look like. At the heart of this new vision was John's Gospel, seen as an authentically Palestinian-Jewish book. Still, he did not at first know what to do with the generally accepted view of John. This Gospel was seen as the most supportive of claims of Jesus' preexistence, as well as the idea that he was God enfleshed and so had always been one with God in the heavenly realm.

Spong undertook a broad study of every aspect of life, including the development of consciousness. He ultimately became open to the concept of a universal consciousness, rather than God in flesh. He began to move away from understanding God as "a being" toward understanding God as "Being itself."

This is heavy stuff, and it led to a new consideration of dimensions of consciousness found in first-century Jewish mysticism.

What followed was an intensive five-year study of John's Gospel. Multiple thousands of pages from multiple sources. The distilled meaning of the commentaries that he studied for us came to this: *John's Gospel is about life—expanded life, abundant life, and ultimately eternal life—but not in the typical manner that these words have been understood religiously . . . I found the Fourth Gospel a book to be lived as much as it was a volume to be mastered.*

Having explained the personal process by which he came to this invitation to consider a new paradigm of Christianity, Bishop Spong concludes his overview chapter with two words of caution and a word of encouragement for those of us who might be bold enough to open our own minds.

First, as noted, John's account cannot be seen as literal. Spong's caution extends to virtually all of the Bible and is echoed by scholars such as Marcus Borg and Karen Armstrong. The volume is a marvelous amalgam of history, myth, allegory, exaggeration, written in changing social and cultural contexts by a plethora of authors, many unknown, each with a particular agenda. The particular caution about literal reading of John's Gospel is reinforced by the knowledge that it was written in layers by different people over a period of about thirty years.

The first caution makes the second self-evident. Although we naturally long for certainty, we will not get it. So much superstition has been laid on the texts of the Bible, and so many fears of men and women have been invested in this book, as people seek a certainty in the Bible, which neither life nor religion can ever provide, that genuine biblical knowledge is hard to attain.

Combining these two warnings with a view of John through the lens of Jewish mysticism led him to see in this Gospel the important role of "signs." All of this produced a conclusion pointing to a new way to understand John's meaning as a part of a New Christianity. That new understanding is at odds with much of standard Christianity on specific matters. Spong found, for example, that many of the characters in John's Gospel are literary or fictional creations of the writers. The language of an external deity entering our physical existence is not even close to what the writers intended.

We should always bear in mind, however, that Spong's tearing down of cherished assumptions is not motivated by a desire to be contrarian for its own sake. Rather, it is to make way for the telling of a new story.

SETTING THE STAGE

Spong closes the chapter with a plea for readers to make the considerable effort that will be required to give fair and open-minded consideration to what he calls *the groundwork for a new way to look at Christianity*. It is no surprise that he recognized this will be difficult. The obstacles are considerable.

A daunting challenge awaits everyone with the courage to seek and apply understanding to the message of a mystic, much less a Jewish mystic. It is the challenge of seeing beyond the capacity of the mind—of going beyond reason. The Western mind is firmly conditioned to react negatively to the word "mysticism." Reason typically rules.

An added layer of difficulty must be faced by those like me who are not writing on a blank slate when it comes to understanding the purpose and message of the historical Jesus. If we are to accept Spong's assertions about these matters as found in John's Gospel, we have a lot of standard religious baggage to unload first.

Spong urges us to make the effort. He does not try to explain in detail how or why accepting his invitation will be worth the considerable effort required because, of course, he cannot. The effect on one's life of a full-scale reconsideration of Christianity is probably the most individualized phenomenon imaginable.

Certainly, I can do no better at convincing you than the author. All I can add is that this way of reconsidering Christianity has probably kept me from casting it aside altogether. That is no small thing. It might do the same for some of you.

CHAPTER 2

John

One Gospel, More Than One Author

BISHOP SPONG'S INTENSIVE STUDY led him to provide further introductory guidance essential to an understanding of New Christianity. First, John's Gospel, indeed the Bible itself, must be understood in the context of the political and social climate that prevailed at the time of the events depicted.

Second, again like most of the Bible, this Gospel was written over time by multiple authors who likely drew on earlier sources. The passage of time may explain the differing, almost contradictory views of Jesus one finds in the book.

For example, in some sections there is no notion that Jesus was always divine. Rather, he is termed the new Moses, the new Elijah, and the like. In others, including the opening passages so troubling to Spong and to me, he is described in supernatural terms as existing before his earthly incarnation.

It is certainly possible to reconcile both of these descriptions. We could see Jesus as "fully human" and "fully divine." Indeed, that is what orthodox Christianity teaches today. Spong's point is that this could not have been the vision of the writers of John. Instead, it is a western concept that developed about three hundred years after the crucifixion.

Further, if we are to see the message of this Gospel as "tales of a Jewish mystic," it is important to understand the next portion of Spong's introductory material. That has to do with sources, one source in particular.

Scholars often look for hidden unacknowledged sources when they examine ancient writings. Many of them saw in John an earlier source called the Book of Signs, on which this Gospel's writers drew heavily. Indeed, they told the larger Jesus story through stories of signs. If true, it explains beginning with the wedding feast in Cana and concluding with the raising of Lazarus.

Spong points out that the sign stories take up almost half of this Gospel. So, as we go through the Gospel, some understanding of how first-century Jews understood a sign is a big key. Here is the bishop's definition, drawn from the Book of Signs:

> ... *a sign is depicted as a mighty act, done quite publicly, that points to something even bigger and more important.*

As the story nears conclusion, however, he will remind us that *signs, however, only point to meanings they cannot finally enfold.*

Spong notes that the stories in John are told in an obscure, enigmatic manner with unusual actions and dramatically drawn characters. He concludes that this mystical style of writing is more evidence that the signs should not be understood as literal events. This in contrast with the uncritical acceptance of the stories as "miracles" in the other three Gospels.

It should be acknowledged here that our reason-oriented Western minds are also capable of reconciling these descriptions of the Gospel stories. But Spong's point is that the several authors who produced John over time simply did not think that way about signs. It was not their purpose to use the stories simply as fodder for metaphor and allegory, useful as that might be. It was not their purpose to offer stories to be unraveled by the exercise of reason. Instead, as we will see, the signs point to a very different conclusion than that espoused by standard Christianity.

Nancy Ford, a retired Anglican Deacon in my area, adapting and paraphrasing the words of author Wendy Wright on a related subject, captured eloquently the problem we have with understanding John:

> We have become skittish about the "invisible reality" that hides beyond the visible ... This may arise from our belief that nothing is true without evidence to support it. Simply put we have lost our willingness to discover mystery and remain open to wonder ... Our fear of that which is considered superstitious ... tends to blind us to the presence of the divine.

PART I | INTRODUCING THE FOURTH GOSPEL

As further evidence that the Gospel is the product of multiple authors over time, Spong confronts one of my favorite stories: Jesus and the woman caught in adultery. It is a story I used in my work against the death penalty. (Believe it or not, prosecutors in capital cases often quoted Scripture, claiming that God had passed on the power over life and death to the state and they were God's messengers. It was sometimes necessary to meet them on their own turf.)

Spong acknowledges the story as a beautiful authentic story of what Jesus could have said but did not. The story was apparently inserted during the Middle Ages. (Even so, I remain thankful for having been able to ask jurors to consider whether they were worthy to cast the first stone.)

Additional evidence, perhaps more theologically significant, includes the fact that the resurrection stories look like unrelated episodes. Finally, as Spong will later explain, there is almost no possibility that the same author wrote chapters 20 and 21.

With this understanding of the social and historical context of events recounted in the Fourth Gospel, Spong tells us that the Gospel will address three distinct episodes in early Christian history and will include an epilogue. This is the background against which he will tell the new story.

The first stage is one deeply related to Jewish synagogues. The time is early- to mid-seventies CE, and Jesus is seen as the fulfillment of Jewish messianic images.

Superimposed on materials about this stage is material that grew out of the increasing hostility between followers of Jesus and the leaders of the Jerusalem synagogue. That division was worsened by the fall of Jerusalem and Roman destruction of the temple in 70 CE. By the year 88, it had led to expulsion of the followers of Jesus from the synagogue. The degree of hostility and recrimination should not be underestimated. It likely exceeded even the schisms of today, including the battle over whether LGBTQ people will be allowed full participation in the modern Christian version of the synagogue.

Unfortunately, this stage produced the most tragic invitation of all to misread John. In this time of mutual vitriol, there are passages with Christians condemning "the Jews." It should not take a biblical scholar to understand that these epithets were not directed at ethnic Jews as such. The Christians involved in this dispute were themselves Jews. Instead, the target was the Jewish temple hierarchy. Nevertheless, whether based in ignorance or cruelty, John became a major source for antisemitism, leading to inquisitions, torture, murder, ghettos, the Holocaust, and beyond. I say beyond because decades after 1945, young Catholic boys can still be heard to call Jews "Christ-killers." Pope Benedict in 2011 was still trying to correct this deadly misreading.

The third stage found in the book's background structure is the most important to our understanding of Spong's New Christianity. It is about a later time when the excommunicated Christians sought to define themselves as separate from the traditional Judaism of which they had always been a part, just as some who adopt the Bishop's New Christianity may define themselves as separate from standard Christianity and its hierarchies.

> *It was in this third editorial phase, I believe, that they began to move into a form of Jewish mysticism that enabled them to reach a new and transcendent sense of the reality of God.*

Unfortunately, later Christians built creeds and dogmas upon even this new understanding, producing a hierarchy similar to the Jewish structure that produced the expulsion of Christians from Judaism.

Consequently, Spong acknowledges that in his book he seeks to excise both antisemitism and creedal authority from Christianity. He asserts that, just as Jewish Christians had to learn to live apart from Judaism, Christians today must learn to live apart from standard creedal Christianity.

Spong here alerts us that in the epilogue he will sum up a radical claim: John's Gospel depicts Jesus as the doorway to experiencing a new dimension of life, a journey into a new consciousness, to a whole new understanding of what Christianity is.

We can see all around us evidence of Spong's further claim that traditional Christianity is dying. His vision of a New Christianity should excite current Christians, intrigue former Christians, and at least spark the interest of the adamantly secular. Particularly for that last group, obtaining at least a rudimentary understanding of spirit will be difficult. My dedicated secular friends are educated and intelligent. They, of course, reject what they see as "religion." But they usually give themselves away by assuming that any proposed discussion will be about what happens when our physical life ends or that the purpose of the discussion will be to recruit them for an organization with a terrible record on human rights. That takes them to a full-throated, sometimes humorous critique of superstition and a devastatingly accurate critique of centuries of organized religion. The subtext is "I am too educated and too smart for this stuff. It is too much work and I don't need it anyway."

Even though my friends miss the point (they miss Spong's by a mile), they must *know* that while our minds can take us a long way, while our reasoning facility can do much good for us and for others, there is something more. Our minds can take us to the threshold but not all the way. How do they know? How do I know? How did Spong know? The answer lies in the real spirit of mysticism. We all erect barriers that keep us from considering or discussing subjects beyond reason. We fear the embarrassment of being seen as superstitious and ignorant. We fear being lumped in with idol worshipers, or worse, the fire and brimstone crowd. But I submit that if one as educated and learned as Bishop John Spong can consider a new way that goes beyond reason, so can we all.

CHAPTER 3

Separating John from the Other Gospels

IN THIS BRIEF CHAPTER, having made his remarkable claim for John as the portal to a new Christianity, Spong provides further introductory matters of importance. He explains how John differs from the other three Gospels, historically and as a literary exercise. He uses these differences to provide some examples of his previous caveats about literal reading and about the twisting of narratives by later religious authorities.

First there is a warning about the "blending" of John with the other Gospels, a feature that characterizes most church services. Anyone with a rudimentary knowledge of a Christian Bible knows that Mark was the earliest Gospel and the authors of Matthew and Luke drew heavily on Mark as their source. This is the reason, the three are called the "Synoptics." (Roughly, "seen with the same eye.") John is the fourth of the Gospels and does not have Mark as a principal source. However, as anyone who has attended the service of any mainstream denomination also knows, these distinctions are not part of the ritual. Instead, the Gospel readings, and indeed many of the important stories, are blended without explanation or context.

Spong sees this willy-nilly blending as a major obstacle to understanding not only John but also each of the other Gospels as well: *One will never understand any Gospel and most especially the Fourth Gospel until the blending process, which actually makes straightforward Bible study all but impossible, is shattered and we can begin to know each Gospel in its uniqueness.*

PART I | INTRODUCING THE FOURTH GOSPEL

The stories he chooses to highlight as examples of blending serve several purposes. First, they emphasize the importance of his repeated warnings against literal reading. The clearest example is the fiction of the "Seven Last Words of Christ" on the cross. Apparently in response to changing social and religious tensions, the writers of the four Gospels deleted phrases found in the others and added their own, including some that sent messages very different from those they deleted. Spong reminds us that

> *the overwhelming probability is that nowhere is there recorded a single word that Jesus actually spoke from the cross.*

Mark, the earliest Gospel, suggests this is because there were no eyewitnesses.

Further examples of what sets John apart and constitutes part of a continuing introduction to radical Christianity include the absence of stories one might expect to find:

- No account of a miraculous virgin birth.
- John the Baptist does not baptize Jesus.
- No account of the temptation of Jesus in the wilderness.
- No parables, no Sermon on the Mount.
- No description of the Last Supper.

Is it not fair to say that these omissions cast a reasonable doubt that at least some of the reported events ever happened at all? John, written in the nineties CE, is the latest account. Why would such important events be omitted? They are included in some but not all of the earlier Gospels.

Finally, in the course of alerting us to the obstacle of blending and to some of the factors that set John's story apart, Spong disputes one of the most significant claims of standard Christianity. He asserts that a physical resurrection and ascension is not the key to the Jesus story. Rather,

> *in The Fourth Gospel Jesus' glorification is portrayed to be the moment of his crucifixion. It is when Jesus is lifted up on the cross that he draws all people to himself. It is not a suffering Christ who is seen on the cross, but a glorified Christ whose work is somehow completed in his death.*

Many elements of the New Christianity Spong finds in John have long been recognized. The Bible translation I use, for example, is the Jerusalem Bible, edited by Dominicans and published in 1966. The commentary preceding

SEPARATING JOHN FROM THE OTHER GOSPELS

John's Gospel acknowledges key differences with the Synoptics, especially around not only the "lifting up" of Christ on the cross as the moment of his glorification but also John's emphasis on the Spirit and the present. The "kingdom" is already here and now and already in possession of those who pass through the doorway of understanding who Jesus is.

Not surprisingly, however, the Dominicans do not go the whole way with Spong. To do so would surely upset Easter. For Spong, if the glorification was the crucifixion, there is no need for physical resurrection and no need for a second coming. The resurrection was instead a dawning of a new consciousness. The title of the book's epilogue reveals the claim: Resurrection Is Not Physical, but It Is Real.

If John's Gospel is indeed markedly different, not necessarily superior or more accurate, etc., but different from the Synoptics, if it offers a new way of relating to God, a new role and purpose for Jesus, then what is it really about?

CHAPTER 4

The Work of a Palestinian Jew

SPONG CONTINUES THE CAMPAIGN to have readers understand John's Gospel in a way that is markedly different from the Synoptics. He urges that, even for those who can get past the standard practice of blending it with the other three Gospels, there is more work to do. That work includes three important guidelines to reading and understanding John:

1. The writers were profoundly influenced by their Jewish experience.
2. The message of the book is significantly shaped by a form of first-century Jewish mysticism.
3. Never read the book literally.

He devotes the remainder of this chapter to the first of these elements. In it, he provides simple scholars of the basics like me with more complex theological observations than we need to know. Consequently, I provide only a brief summary and analysis.

The Jewishness of this Gospel is an important factor to Spong. He contends that *one must develop Jewish eyes, I believe, if one is to understand the Fourth Gospel.* He refers to the writers' numerous references to images from Jewish Scriptures and, of real significance, to the relationship between the way the writers tell the Jesus story and the Jewish liturgical calendar with which they would have been intimately familiar.

His lengthy exposition of evidence for the Jewishness of the book, however, seems to stem mainly from a real concern about the influence of Hellenistic philosophy in complicating a uniquely Jewish narrative. He acknowledges that some of this was unavoidable. Greek was the formal language of the entire Roman Empire at the time. Virtually all of the original documents that became the New Testament were written in Greek. When writing in Greek, he observes, one necessarily absorbs Greek concepts and is unconsciously shaped by a Greek worldview.

Add to this that the early community of Christians finally turned away from Judaism and embraced Hellenism, and one can appreciate why Spong sees John's Gospel as the primary bridge that connected the two traditions. He is not overly troubled about that development in itself. It was what happened after the Gospels were written that is of great concern.

As the early church drew more and more gentile members, the Hebrew tradition, so essential to understanding John, disappeared. The Gospels came to be interpreted by a church hierarchy composed of people who were ignorant of Hebrew traditions and customs. This in turn produced the standard Christianity most of us know, as well as the creeds that have produced so much harm in the world.

The transition to new Greek interpretations reached a new and dominant height by the fourth century, when creeds were being written and the theological images that would dominate classical Christianity were being formed.

The most troubling of those theological images, the ones most influenced by Greek thought, the ones most in need of the now lost Hebrew tradition were those found in the prologue to John. It is to that subject that Spong turns in his next chapter.

CHAPTER 5

Tracing the Jewish Roots of the Prologue

> "In the beginning was the Word: The Word was with God and the Word was God."
>
> JOHN 1:1

THE OPENING VERSES OF John's Gospel are perceived as bedrock in orthodox Christianity. Spong cannot be correct if the "Word" that was up there with God at the creation of the world was really Jesus, who showed up on earth much later. If that is really the message of all the Gospels, then the standard narrative about Jesus flows easily from this story: he was with God all along. He came down to earth and offered himself up as a sacrifice to save only everyone who believed in him from their sins and guarantee their future after they died. His human body was physically resurrected and returned "up there" to be with God again. He will return to claim his believers.

Upon this view, the Christian hierarchy constructed its damaging creeds two to three centuries after the death of Jesus. Upon this view, they claimed authority from God to accept those who adhered to this narrative and also to persecute, torture, and kill those who did not. Worse, there came to be enough different interpretations within this basic story that Christians could even be moved to persecute, torture, and kill one another.

Such is one very basic aspect of the history of Christianity, and the prologue to John's Gospel is perceived as an important part of it. Such also is the Christianity that so many have tried and rejected, or never tried at all. Who can blame them?

Given this profound impact, it is little wonder that Bishop Spong had to devote two chapters to explaining another way to read the prologue to the Fourth Gospel. His examination is, similar to some of that found in the previous chapter, a bit scholarly. Bearing in mind that our objective is not to become theologians but rather to understand a New Christianity, I will try to simplify both this and the chapter that follows.

Spong asks rhetorically: *Why would a Jewish author write such a non-Jewish-sounding prologue?* One answer proffered in scholarly circles is that the prologue was not part of the Gospel at all but rather an addition by a writer with a different agenda. True to his warning to us that this Gospel must be read with Jewish eyes, he adopts a second reason: the prologue really is in keeping with Jewish tradition. It has simply been misunderstood and reshaped by gentile-trained eyes, also with a dollop of antisemitism.

The key to Spong's analysis is "the Word." He compares the prologue with the Genesis creation myth and concludes that the anonymous writers who produced the Genesis story attributed enormous power to the Word, which was separate from God but of God's very essence.

Western thinking, influenced by the Greeks, uses the term "logos" for the Word. But the Hebrew word is *dabar*. The concept of dabar was that it had power to shape the world, to reveal the presence of God, and to call people to a heightened sense of selfhood, a higher consciousness. As we will see, this concept will be fundamental to a new vision of Christianity and a counterweight to the gentile-created orthodoxy.

To be sure, like most ancient people, Jews located God somewhere beyond the sky. But they also saw God as both transcendent (external) and immanent (existing or operating within). Note that standard Christian doctrine attempts to reconcile these two by requiring that believers see Jesus as "fully human" and simultaneously "fully divine." That would of course be consistent with the vision of the divine Jesus being up there with God at the beginning of the world, coming down and assuming human form, and going back up with the promise of returning later.

PART I | INTRODUCING THE FOURTH GOSPEL

Spong has a different interpretation. He traces the evolution of the Jewish view of God's Word in the history of Judaism through the time of Moses to Judges to Kings. We know that some of that history was an effort to give God an earthly location, namely, a temple. Summarizing the story, he notes that *like all people, Jews would have to learn that God cannot be possessed, nor can "the Word" be reduced to propositional statements.* Incidentally, that same lesson would eventually come from the prophets, not from the Jewish hierarchy.

Spong also identifies a truth that is essential to a new understanding of God, Jesus, and the Word. It is a truth common to Jew and gentile alike: *while God may not be subject to change, the human experience of God is, and history, even the history of the Bible, is the story of the ever-changing human perceptions of God.*

Keeping that in mind can produce an entirely new understanding of the Bible and reveal its relevance in ways that the standard use of Scripture in churches simply cannot.

In respect of the prologue, an illustration is the changing perception in Jewish history from the early vengeful tribal god to the universal god found in the book of Malachi, then on to the concept of a Messiah rather than a king as God's anointed one, a Messiah who taught about loving one's enemies. All these diverse perceptions were set out by Jewish writers. By the time of the Jewish writers of John's Gospel, the God whose representative was portrayed in the earlier Gospels bore little or no resemblance to the tribal war God who sponsored the brutal conquest of Canaan.

Spong writes, however, that Jews still thought of God as an *external being* and that left them with the age-old longing for oneness with the creator. Jewish thought, he says, had to go through one more transformation before the words of the prologue could be written and their real meaning understood. That would happen when the view of God as an external being was challenged by the coming of a new understanding of the *immanence* of God, the *permeating presence* of God. The challenge would develop through the rise of what is known as wisdom literature and Jewish mysticism. These are explored and explained in the following chapter.

CHAPTER 6

Permeating Wisdom

The Doorway to Jewish Mysticism

WHEN THE WRITERS OF the final Gospel were expelled from the synagogue, they and all the Johannine Christians were in a real sense freed. They were freed from the narrow compulsory narrative that the religious hierarchy insisted upon. They were free to explore themes that are more universal as a way to tell their Jesus story.

In a beautiful irony, the vision that emerged beyond Mosaic law then also gives us today a way to go beyond the very similar narrative of standard Christianity. The expulsion of Johannine Christians from the synagogue turned out to be a blessing for everyone.

Again, Spong recognizes the obstacle of our aversion to mysticism. He opens the chapter with the observation that mysticism is part of every religious system, but its place is on the fringe of acceptability.

Recognizing that mysticism is always in some sense a commentary on the adequacy of traditional definitions, we can see that our reason deposits us on its doorstep. What lies within is worth exploring for the very practical, life-enhancing results that it can produce. The further explanation of how to understand the prologue to John's Gospel invites us also to a greater understanding of spirit.

The use of newly acquired freedom, however, can be affected by time and circumstances. Spong contends that the Gospel of John was tragically distorted by the early Christian authorities, who were Greek thinkers with little understanding of anything Jewish, certainly none of Jewish mysticism. It was they who produced the damaging creeds. Steeped in Greek thought, they were dualists who saw souls and bodies, spiritual things and material things, as sometimes antagonistic separate realms. And so, the prologue to John came to be preached as the basis for the creed that Jesus was always up there ("begotten not made; being of one substance with the Father, by whom all things are made"); that he came down and died to save us from our sins ("for us and for our salvation he came down from heaven . . . was crucified for us under Pontius Pilate"); and that he went back up there but will return (to "judge both the quick and the dead").

But freedom means that both we and John's early Christians can consider the prologue differently. Spong begins with the simple contention that *Jesus was not Clark Kent.*

So, if we are free to consider the Gospel of John, including the prologue, differently, what was the difference in the way its writers told the Jesus story? Spong is satisfied that it was by use of Jewish mysticism and the anteroom of mysticism was Jewish Wisdom literature.

Before explaining that transition, however, he reminds us of the point he made in the previous chapter. A mystical account is going to reflect a changing God, or a changing human perception of God. But God has never been static in human history. People have always adapted their understanding of God to the realities of their lives. Human beings always create God in their own image to meet their own needs. This statement brings to mind a familiar trope of intellectual skeptics to the effect that if there were no God, people would invent one. Spong does not address this directly, but my thought is that this assertion of skeptics is simplistic and incomplete. They omit recognition of the possibility that there might be a God, one who can meet the real needs of people whenever and wherever they are. And the meeting of those needs is in truth facilitated by an evolving image of God's identity and nature.

Building on that changing vision of God, Spong explains the process by which the Jewish understanding of God evolved from that of a distant dictator of laws—the Torah—to Wisdom writings: God as immanent, personal. And finally, a mystical vision of oneness:

> . . . *a form of Jewish mysticism became the lens through which the final writing of the gospel was to be read. To say that "the word was made flesh" is to say that in the life of Jesus people saw the will of God being lived out and they heard the word of God being spoken.*

PERMEATING WISDOM

> *To exhort people to be born again or to be born of the spirit... was not to call them to a conversion experience that would make them superior to others; rather it was to invite them to escape life's limits and enter a new level of consciousness where they would begin to see themselves as part of who God is and to experience God as part of who they are... It was that mystical oneness that enabled Johannine followers of Jesus to perceive Jesus as part of who God is.*

This notion of our oneness with God can be found in other traditions. The Unity movement and New Thought are examples. But it forms part of a radical New Christianity because the understanding of God it expresses is quite different from "Holy Trinity" or "God in three persons."

Spong, having devoted sixty-one pages to preparing readers to consider the Gospel of John in a very new way, still sees the need for a final caution about religious literalism before taking us through the Gospel stories. I think this final caution was a good idea. Religious literalism is not only spiritually misleading; it is also causing real harm to real people of many faiths, as well as to those of no faith.

CHAPTER 7

John the Non-Literalist

Spong's caution against literalism in the final introductory chapter is far from an afterthought. Indeed, as a trial lawyer, I see its placement as an example of the principle of primacy and recency. The last thing a jury hears has the greatest impact. And Spong makes sure in this chapter to get the undivided attention of the reader by including some of the most radical assertions of New Christianity.

The chapter begins with a plain-spoken reminder of the weaknesses of literal reading of the Gospel as opposed to trying to understand it as a product of Jewish mysticism:

> *Mysticism expands words beyond their normal limits and calls the mystic into the ultimate experience of wordlessness. The best words can do is to point beyond themselves to a new reality that words can never contain or even describe.*
>
> *Literalism commits us to the presumption that any religious form can not only capture truth, but also explain it fully.*

Spong then provides examples that he openly confesses are designed to be provocative. He contends that these startling assertions are all grounded in the preponderance of biblical scholarship. He is one of a small group that can be trusted when that claim is made.

JOHN THE NON-LITERALIST

The attack on literalism is on two fronts. The first, as previously noted, is that many events set out in the Gospel just never happened on the ground. Among a long list he provides:

- No water was ever turned into wine at Cana.
- Jesus never raised a man named Lazarus from the dead.
- There never was a triumphal entry to Jerusalem.
- Jesus never identified his body with the temple or likened his flesh to bread and his blood to wine.
- We have no idea what, if anything, Jesus said from the cross.

What happens when these are assumed to be actual events is to confuse storytelling and parable with history.

And Spong also makes it clear that he is not only speaking to today's fundamentalist Christians who try to tell us that every word given to us by a commission appointed by an English king actually came down directly from God. He goes on to address Catholics, Anglicans, Episcopalians, and indeed all who consider themselves too intelligent to accept the King James version completely literally.

Some of us pick and choose our literalism. We look down our collective noses when we point out some of the obvious contradictions and flaws in a literal reading of Scripture, but we draw the line when it comes to the virgin birth or the physical resurrection, or some other biblical event that we see as important. What if those did not happen either?

The second attack on literalism is more nuanced. It is also directed at the educated and sophisticated among us who understand the concept of metaphor and allegory. Inviting use of these devices is one of the Bible's blessings. We can be spiritually enriched by envisioning new and different metaphors and comparisons and relating them to our times. But that is as far as many of us get in rejecting literalism. And that cannot take us to full understanding of the mystical meaning of John's Gospel. This is true of another list of examples Spong uses to discredit literalism:

- The encounter with Jesus shows Nicodemus, an educated Jew, as one who is cautiously curious but who simply cannot overcome literalism. He goes away sadly, unable to understand beyond the literal meaning of being born again.

- Similarly, the Samaritan woman at the well at first cannot comprehend *living water* and tells Jesus he doesn't even have a bucket.
- Following this meeting, we see that even the disciples cannot grasp Jesus' offer of food to eat "of which you do not know."

To be sure, fundamentalists and indeed virtually all traditional denominations do not always take these examples literally. They see different metaphors for new birth, living water, and spiritual food. But Spong contends that the Johannine Christians had a different and even deeper perspective when they told the Jesus story. Scriptures point to truth but they cannot capture it. John should not be read literally, or even solely as an invitation to additional inspiring metaphors and allegories. Rather, it is a book of signs with repeated lessons about mystical truths.

We should pause here to recognize unashamedly the universal value of the Bible. One of its many wonders, in any translation, is its gift of ambiguity. It came to the world through a hodgepodge of writers, editors, and languages—all with an effect on the meaning and value of the text. Most of what Christians call the New Testament, for example, came to us from texts written in Greek, a language Jesus did not speak. Its very vagueness enables it to serve as a beneficial life guide for many who try to read it literally, as well as many others who gain similar guidance from seeing different metaphors in the stories. The fundamentalist Christians I have mentioned, for example, can also go beyond the physical literalism of "born again" and see a requirement that we all be allegorically reborn into followers of Jesus as the one who can save us from the consequences of our sins. Neither Spong nor I see "born again" that way, but we respect that path.

New Christianity has more to offer. It is not just about taking tentative steps beyond literalism. It is about a greater understanding of the life, purpose, and message of Jesus, as seen by the writers and editors of John through the lens of Jewish mysticism. It is about a new level of consciousness, a new dimension of what it means to be human. Explanation of this vision is contained in the remainder of the book. He introduces it briefly in this chapter:

> *This gospel is not about God becoming human, about God putting on flesh and masquerading as a human being; it is about bringing God out of the sky and redefining God as the ultimate dimension of the human. It is about seeing Jesus as the doorway into a new consciousness, which is also a doorway into God, who might be perceived as a universal consciousness.*

JOHN THE NON-LITERALIST

In fairness to traditional Christianity, it must be admitted that the more progressive denominations do not reject these views outright. There is room for discussion and debate within their theological circles. The problem is that getting beyond literalism to considering the transformational impact on our lives flowing from a vision of God as the ultimate dimension of the human is almost never presented to the Sunday congregation. It is not that the traditional understanding has no value at all. It is that the exciting new and different vision of a small community of Jewish Christians is a light truly being hidden under a bushel.

One of the characters in John who is a purposeful literary creation is found at the opening of John's Gospel. Nathaniel, whose name means "the gift of God," is brought to Jesus by Philip, and it is Jesus himself who brings him to discipleship to become one of the twelve apostles. Nathaniel is not only not listed as such in the other Gospels; he is not even mentioned.

Spong sees Nathaniel as a symbol to help explain the position of the early Johannine Christians in relation to official Judaism. His exchange with Jesus depicts Nathaniel as open-minded but skeptical. It is significant that Jesus also identifies him as one who has diligently studied the Torah. In the conclusion of their brief encounter, Nathaniel recognizes Jesus as the Son of God and the King of Israel about whom he has been studying. Jesus replies that Nathaniel will see even greater things. Seen not as a historical figure but as a literary device, Nathaniel thus provides context for the situation in which the community that produced this Gospel found itself—and the Jesus story it would produce.

With all this in mind, we are now ready to examine the Fourth Gospel in detail. We will see not only a little-known telling of the Jesus story but also the outline of a new and exciting way of incorporating the story into our lives.

PART II

The Book of Signs
Mythological Characters Wrapped Inside History

CHAPTER 8

The Mother of Jesus

Introduction to the Book of Signs

THE CHAPTER THAT FINALLY takes us into the John's Gospel text is worth the wait. It features the Book of Signs, which may have been circulating separately. Spong is endeavoring to educate us about a new way to read and understand a single book. But he also begins here to reveal much more about Bible-reading itself and about the larger vision of a New Christianity that arises from a new understanding of the Jesus story.

In this new exposition one can discern the distinction between signs and the interpretive allegories and metaphors we are all free to envision and create when we read biblical stories. As noted, the very contradictions and ambiguity in the stories are a gift. The numerous writers and editors, many unknown, all with their own agendas and interpretations, give us the opportunity to see beyond the literal to interpretations that are helpful in our daily lives. The absence of a consistent definitive narrative frees us to walk our own path, educated and inspired in our own way, as we try to figure out life and perhaps form a relationship with what some call God.

But signs are something more. Something beyond. Not just inspirational aphorisms, the signs in John are part of a coherent narrative revealing a radical new purpose for the Jesus story—one that is consistent with love and inconsistent with the rigid literalism that forms the basis for so much harm to people. It is that freedom from literalism that distinguishes these signs from the misguided narrative that characterizes much of apocryphal writings. As Spong repeatedly insists, signs must be viewed through a mystical lens. Doing so gives us an even greater gift.

As also noted, one factor hindering the understanding of any of the Gospels as coherent narrative is that the liturgies of standard Christianity, Protestant and Catholic, provide followers only with disjointed snippets of one Gospel or another. This gives the impression that all the Gospels are alike.

It also leaves the explanations to the clergy in charge, and that does not bode well for understanding the mystical message of John. Neither does it give us any idea that there is a new and radical way to understand the Jesus story that just may be better for us and the world. That vision is kept away from congregations and safely ensconced within the confines of high theological discourse.

In John, the well-known story of Jesus changing water to wine at a wedding feast in Cana provides the first sign. This is not a miracle story. Rather, it is the point of introduction to the first of the themes that reflect the Gospel writers' understanding of the nature and purpose of the life of Jesus and of his relationship with God.

As we will see, this exposition of a New Christianity will continue to topple the icons of the old—beginning here with the use and misuse of the mother of Jesus in standard Christianity.

In this story, the principal characters are Jesus and his mother. She is not called Mary. There is no suggestion that she was a virgin. She appears only once more in the New Testament, at the foot of the cross. Because of what the Catholic Church in particular has done with this character over the years, Spong sees it as important to de-literalize her story in order to have it understood the way the writers of John intended. To do so, he notes, also requires something other than a literal understanding of the birth narratives found in Matthew and Luke, inspiring though they may be.

The mother of Jesus in the Cana wedding story is a mythological figure and had been such in early Christian writings long before John's Gospel appeared. John continues to develop the myth by building into his characterization of her the things he needs her to be and do in order to develop his story.

Spong bolsters this characterization of Mary by reference to the writings of Paul that appeared before any Gospel and decades before Matthew and Luke. In that earliest writing, Paul makes no mention at all of the parents of Jesus. He does refer to James as the brother of Jesus and to

Jesus himself as being "born of a woman." And, of course, neither Paul nor Mark set out any accounts of mangers, wise men, travels, etc.

The Cana wedding story is well known, at least in Christian circles. It is a brief, twelve-verse account of a wedding feast that ran out of wine for the guests. The mother of Jesus told him about it, and he replied by asking her why she was bothering him about it since "my hour has not come yet." She then told the servants to do anything her son might ask. Jesus told the them to fill six stone water jars, each able to hold twenty to thirty gallons. They did, and what they drew out was excellent wine. This was the first sign that allowed the glory of Jesus to be seen. Afterward, he and his mother and brothers left for Capernaum.

To understand this story as a sign, it is necessary to do even more than go beyond literalizing it. Again, what is the difference between a sign and the metaphors and allegories we are all able to construct when we go beyond literalism? It is to use symbols and literary characters to do more than fashion creative and useful interpretations. It is to use these devices in service of a broader coherent narrative that reveals an entirely new vision. The Cana wedding story is not a standalone parable.

This path to a new understanding does not deny the value of the old. Rather, only the authority and exclusivity of the old.

It should be heartening to see this as other than a miracle story. Being able to pull off a physical miracle is no small matter, to be sure. But if that is all miracles are, their value to us is limited. He performed a miracle: "Yay, Jesus! But I don't have a wine cellar, and I can't afford to go to parties. What do I do now about my empty cupboard and my soaring grocery bills?"

How can we see the Cana story as not only metaphorical but also mystical? Spong argues that in the story Jesus is clearly the bridegroom who is calling Israel to a new status. And if we recognize that 150 gallons of new and excellent wine were provided, we can see that this new life will be one of overwhelming abundance. *The wine of the spirit has replaced the waters of purification.* Mary, "the mother of the Lord" is a mythological figure who stands for Israel, the faith tradition that gave birth to Christianity and thus its mother.

But when will this call to a new Israel, this transition, be answered? We only learn from this story that the hour has not yet come. But we get a hint of the rest of the story when Spong reminds us that the next time the symbolic figure of the mother of Jesus appears is at the foot of the cross.

CHAPTER 9

Nicodemus

What It Means to be Born of the Spirit

HERE WE FIND THE story of Jesus and a mythological character, one Nicodemus. The story has much to teach us about literalism, educated skeptics, and most importantly, a further introductory outline of a New Christianity.

It is interesting that the chapter opens with only a very brief mention of the next event set out in the Gospel, the well-known story of Jesus driving the money changers from the temple. Spong connects it with the Nicodemus episode only by saying they are examples of Jesus trying to teach that the new will replace the old. The temple stands for his body, and when this sanctuary is destroyed, he will raise it up in three days. The standard Christian understanding of this statement is that it is a reference to his death and physical resurrection. Spong sees the statement quite differently but chooses not to elaborate here.

The inability of the character Nicodemus to understand the famous saying of Jesus that he must be born again reminds us that even those who claim to take the Bible literally have to make exceptions. Not even the most dedicated fundamentalist would have responded as Nicodemus did: "How is that possible? Can he go back into his mother's womb and be born again?"

There is much more to learn from this exchange and how John drew the character of Nicodemus. We are told he was a Pharisee, a well-educated leading Jew. Secure and comfortable in a world that had nothing to do with Jesus, he nevertheless sought him out, albeit secretly. He even referred to Jesus as rabbi and said he knew that Jesus was a teacher who came from God.

Something had moved Nicodemus. And something moves some of us today. We somehow know there is more. There is no incentive to embrace it, and there is some risk. We are doing just fine without the risk. But we decide nevertheless to cautiously inquire further. Alas, after that tentative first step something causes us, like Nicodemus, to step back. Perhaps it is the comfort of the current situation; perhaps it is the risk of abandoning our security structures; perhaps it is simply the inability to expand our understanding from literal to mystical.

Alas, perhaps that was the reason Nicodemus eventually walked away, retreating to the security of his orthodox Judaism.

Much is the pity also for those of us who take a first step and then retreat to safety. For in this chapter is found a more detailed introduction to what we miss, what the New Christianity is all about—what Jesus was trying to get through to Nicodemus.

Surprisingly, as we shall see in the story of the crucifixion, Nicodemus came back. Although we do not know how he ultimately resolved his inner struggle to be free of limits, it appears in John's story that he was drawn back to the powerful words Jesus had spoken to him. Perhaps an invitation to former Christians today to look again also?

We have already seen that even as he gradually reveals the New Christianity envisioned by the authors of John, Spong continues to dismantle traditional Christianity. Consequently, I was quite surprised to find that he did not continue that criticism to any degree in this chapter. After all, the conversation with Nicodemus contains what may be the most famous verse in the New Testament, the King James Version of John 3:16.

Watch a televised sporting event in the United States and, in addition to signs supporting a team, you will very often see one simply reading "John 3:16." There is even a popular country music song with the line "all I know is 3:16." This misunderstood verse, along with verse 18 and the equally misread John 14:6, form the bedrock summary of the "sin and salvation" narrative that characterizes all of standard Christianity, especially the fundamentalist branches. Here is the way King James I's scholarly committee translated the verses:

PART II | THE BOOK OF SIGNS

> For God so loved the world, that he gave his only begotten Son that whosoever believeth in him should not perish, but have everlasting life. (John 3:16)

> He that believeth in him is not condemned: but he that believeth not is condemned already, because he hath not believed in the name of the only begotten Son of God. (John 3:18)

> I am the way, the truth and the life: no man cometh unto the father, but by me. (John 14:6)

For millions, this is the source of those divisive creeds, of the "us vs. them" exceptionalism; of the narrative of afterlife for the true believers and eternal damnation for non-believers.

Spong must have found it supremely ironic that these passages appear only in the Gospel that he claimed was telling of a completely different way, a completely different understanding of truth and life; indeed, a completely new understanding of the Jesus story. I wish I had had a chance to ask him about that.

Instead of undertaking the relatively easy task of debunking the dominant understanding of John 3:16 et seq. directly, he makes a different choice. We see that undermining the story of salvation from sin by a visitor from above will be intertwined with a counternarrative, and both will unfold gradually.

Upon reflection, I view that as a wise choice. It certainly makes for a more compelling story.

There is indeed some criticism of standard Christianity in this chapter. But more importantly, it is in the explanation that John was writing as a Jewish mystic, not a Greek rationalist, that we learn much about the New Christianity:

Spong claims that Jesus was speaking to Nicodemus about a new dimension of life, not a new religious experience: that Jesus was indeed from another realm, but it is *a realm that must be understood experientially, not spatially.*

To be "born of the spirit," in contrast to birth into the life of this world, is to step into *a new dimension of what it means to be human.*

These words, of course, constitute an implicit refutation of the common understanding of the doctrine built around John 3:16. Perhaps as important, the repeated use of the word "dimension" is a reminder of the difficulty of transcending the rational, something poor Nicodemus was unable to accomplish.

Spong concludes the chapter by alluding to what is called Jewish "throne mysticism." He finds that in John's Gospel the glory of Christ, his "enthronement," was on the cross not in a physical resurrection, a return to the sky, or a coming again. *That instrument of execution will provide a doorway into a new consciousness, a new oneness with all that God is, a doorway into that which is eternal. Jesus is the source of love that comes to open the eyes of people to see that they are part of who and what God is.*

Leaving this encounter with one whose initial courage could not overcome his rational cost-benefit assessment, we now move to another revealing conversation.

CHAPTER 10

The Samaritan Woman at the Well

A New Dimension of the Jesus Experience

JOHN'S CREATION OF THE conversation between Jesus and the woman at the well reveals an important component of New Christianity that is ignored or even opposed by many adherents to standard Christianity: radical inclusion. The chapter also goes beyond the "celestial visitor" image of Jesus and tells us more about who the writers of John thought this person was and why he was here.

The introduction to the story tells us that John the Baptist was continuing to baptize, and there was a sort of competition with disciples of Jesus who were also baptizing—and they were winning. As John the Baptist cleared this up, we see once again the theme of a wedding, a bonding, a union. John casts Jesus as the bridegroom and himself as a sort of "best man." He concedes that as Jesus grows greater, he himself will grow smaller, and he is quite content with that. The reason, as Spong understands the words attributed to John the Baptist, is this: *Jesus is the dispenser of the spirit, which means that because the spirit links us to that which is the source of life, Jesus is the doorway into that life which is eternal.* Again and again, we will see Spong use the image of Jesus as a doorway, a doorway to something quite different from the doctrines of standard Christianity.

All this is a lead-in to the conversation at the well. There we are told more about who Jesus is by means of a lesson in radical inclusion.

THE SAMARITAN WOMAN AT THE WELL

The wedding trope is continued, albeit in an understated way, by setting the conversation at a well. Wells were important to the distinctly Jewish stories of how Isaac came to wed Rebekah, Jacob found Rachel, and Moses came to marry Zipporah. A well was the place to go when searching for a wife. That is the context that this symbolic woman would have understood when she came to draw water and Jesus asked for a drink. She would eventually find that Jesus was seeking to be the unifier of families that a bridegroom is but certainly not in the way she initially understood!

The brilliantly powerful component of this story is the casting of the woman as a Samaritan. Even many not raised in Christianity are familiar with the parable of the "good Samaritan" who helped an injured person when others had ignored him as they passed by. Many jurisdictions today have "good Samaritan" laws protecting those who stop to render aid. Some who know the Bible story are even aware that the basis of the parable is that Jews and Samaritans did not particularly care for one another.

There is much more than that to the hostility between Jews and Samaritans. Their enmity speaks to us across the centuries and resembles many of the destructive divisions we all face today. In the story, when Jesus asks the woman at the well for a drink, she immediately reminds him of that bitter history. The depth of that hostility is so important that Spong interrupts the story to provide some details.

Samaritans were the product of a bitter split of one Jewish kingdom into two around 920 BCE. They were Jews, but were part of the Northern Kingdom of Israel, whose rulers built a capital, Samaria. They hoped it would rival Jerusalem, capital of the Southern Kingdom of Judah. The northerners also tried to build a royal family that would rival the famed house of David.

Many of the consequences of that division are familiar today. Secession led to violence and war, to ill-advised alliances with other powers. Much blood was shed. Worse, each of the two sides considered themselves the "chosen people," so they naturally hated anyone else with the audacity to assume that label. Each side began to define itself primarily in terms of something about the other that it was not. Predictably, just as artificial and divisive designations do today, this variant of "identity politics" developed into a form of racism.

This division had tragic consequences when both kingdoms were conquered by foreign powers. First, the people of Israel were exiled for a time after the kingdom was conquered by the Assyrians. They assimilated and intermarried. In contrast, when the people of Judah were later defeated by the forces of Babylon and also exiled, they took great pains to remain separate from Babylonian society. It was here that they adopted rigid observance of Sabbath, strict dietary laws, and the requirement of circumcision. They saw this as consistent with the history that had been passed down to them. In what Christians call the Old Testament, one finds God himself sternly warning the people to remain separate. When they returned from Babylon, the few Judaeans who had intermarried even obeyed orders to put away their wives and children.

Thus, it is not difficult to understand that those who had remained "purely Jewish" referred to the Northern Kingdom Samaritans as a "mongrel race."

Back to the well. The conclusion of the story is brilliantly drawn. The Gospel writers reveal vital aspects of the New Christianity that Jesus is bringing. In the story they show how going beyond literalism reveals Jesus as the Messiah, the Way-Shower to a new dimension of radical, loving inclusion.

Predictably, when Jesus tells the woman that he offers "living water" which would end thirst, the woman's literalism initially keeps her from understanding. At one point she even reminds him that that he doesn't have a bucket! But she does eventually understand, after Jesus says "It is the 'I AM' who is speaking to you now."

One of the better-known aspects of this mythical conversation is Jesus telling the woman about her five husbands, not counting the man she was living with at the time. This part of the story is commonly misunderstood as being about sexual immorality. Instead, beyond literalism and seen through the eyes of a Jewish mystic, it is part of the gospel of radical loving inclusion, again understandable from the history of the Jew/Samaritan split with which she would be familiar.

Spong reminds us: *At this point people forget that the woman is a mythological symbol of Samaria . . . This is a symbolic conversation about how the unfaithful region of Samaria can be incorporated into the new understanding of Christianity and about how ancient religious divisions in the human family can be overcome in the new human consciousness that Jesus comes to bring.*

He explains that the five husbands stand for people of five countries referred to in the book of 2 Kings. During the period of subservience to Assyria, people from five countries were brought to the cities of Samaria. Instead of remaining faithful to their God, the Samaritans bonded with the false gods of the five nations. This error was part of the schism with the southern Jews.

But now, Samaria was to be part of the new Israel. No one was to be excluded. The story is about God taking us beyond human divides, and human prejudices.

The story has a powerful ending. Unlike Nicodemus the educated Jew, a Pharisee no less, the almost certainly less educated woman at the well gets it! She understands! Unlike Nicodemus, she is able to get beyond literalism. She is able to make a commitment that Nicodemus simply could not. Perhaps her lower station in life made it easier for her to do that. Perhaps, having less of what the material world offered, she was better able to comprehend the spiritual.

Whatever the reason, the mission to the Samaritans is now in the hands of a woman, meaning that another barrier to oneness in the human family is being overcome. And we are told that she was quite successful in her new ministry.

The disciples, as is often the case with us, were slower on the uptake. They marveled that Jesus was talking with a woman. They worried that he had not eaten. This prompted him to give them their own spiritual lesson about going beyond literalism when he explained the meaning of his statement that he had "food to eat that you do not know about."

Spong concludes: *Jesus is a barrier-breaker. Before him falls the human division first between Jews and Samaritans and then between men and women.* The message to us is also clear. We cannot abide any division based on sex, gender, color, form of government, etc. Oneness is a challenging, awe-inspiring concept.

This little story not only conveys an important dimension of a New Christianity of radical inclusion; it also helps us understand what is meant by trying to see the stories through the eyes of a Jewish mystic.

Next, John tells us more about inclusion and its incompatibility with standard religion. It is all in a tale about another unnamed character: a gentile official.

CHAPTER 11

The Gentile Official's Son

The Meaning of God and Faith

AN EVEN MORE POWERFUL revelation of a New Christianity is packed into a mere twelve verses of the Gospel's fourth chapter. Those who have not yet escaped literalism may see here merely another account of Jesus performing a miraculous healing. Read through the lens of Jewish mysticism, however, the story reveals much more about radical inclusion, a radical new understanding of God, and the nature of faith.

Returning to Cana where he had changed water to wine, Jesus encounters someone described only as an official from Capernaum. The similarity of this story to those in other Gospels suggests that the official is a gentile. If that quite plausible assumption is correct, Jesus can now be seen as expanding the concept of radical inclusion to include all the world. It is one thing to unite Jews and Samaritans who shared common ancestors but had been at each other's throats for centuries. That is remarkable. But what of the line of demarcation that by definition separates all Jews and non-Jews?

Spong outlines in detail how Jews throughout their history have survived by keeping themselves separate. He notes the general success of this survival tactic. Jews, living as strangers in someone else's country, survived for 1,800 years. In contrast, where are the Edomites, Moabites, Philistines, etc.?

THE GENTILE OFFICIAL'S SON

But Jews have paid a price for that separation. Indeed, the fear that gentiles have of people who are "different" has stoked antisemitism over the centuries. The struggle over if and how Jews and gentiles could be Christians dominated the early days of Christianity. Jewish laws and practices designed to foster a separate identity contributed to the divisiveness. Centuries later, respected Jewish historian Hannah Arendt drew criticism for tracing how Jewish isolation contributed to the Holocaust.

Yet here is this gentile official somehow deciding to plead with an itinerant Jew for help because his son is dying. What drove him to this desperate act? Spong says that *throwing caution to the wind, he crossed the tribal divide.*

The official begs Jesus to come to his home and cure his son. Jesus replies by asking whether the man requires signs and portents in order to believe. The official either does not understand or does not have time for theological debate. He repeats, "Sir, come down before my child dies!"

Here the story of bridging the gulf between Jew and gentile is skillfully blended with an introduction to the mystical nature of God. Jesus simply says, "Go, your son lives." He does not go to the man's home. He does not come in contact with the sick child. The official's servants meet him on the road back to his home with the good news that the fever has left the child at the moment of the pronouncement by Jesus. But . . . we are told that the official had already "believed" before he got this news. He believed without seeing the proof, or even hearing any evidence. He, and gentiles, had been included in a new vision of Christianity.

Life calls to life. Love calls to love . . . and in that understanding the separation of Jew from gentile also quite clearly disappears.

This remote healing was also a sign that God was present in Jesus but was not confined to his single life. The presence of God could not be bound to a particular time and space. God was (and is) a mystical presence permeating the world.

These characterizations of God as a "mystical presence permeating the world," and the assertion that God's location cannot be bounded, are stunning components of New Christianity. Spong compares them with the standard understanding. He explains that once we defined God as a particular being, what was then required was to construct the means of controlling God. First, we had to locate God in a place. We decided that was up in the sky. Then we had to build earthly dwelling places for God, i.e., churches, temples, synagogues. What followed then was that God's words to us could be captured in sacred writings. The control mechanism that naturally followed was to take the words of those writings and construct creeds, dogmas, and prescribed liturgies. Those who didn't conform might at one time literally be burned at the stake. The burning is figurative today. Testament to that is pious exclusion of LGBTQ people and loud silence when church zealots engage in more threatening practices.

That is the essence of standard religion, and it certainly cannot work with a God who is "a mystical presence permeating the world." It was a presence that in this story healed a very sick child and gladdened the heart of one who loved him enough to cross the divide between Jew and gentile.

But Spong's purpose is not only to deconstruct standard Christianity, but also to present a new and beautiful alternative. Anyone seeking to do that must deal with the ascendence of reason and science over the centuries. Those developments are at the heart of why so many people now reject what they see as "religion." The implicit assumption is that they, and indeed the world, are too intelligent for any faith path.

The rise of reason and science has surely dealt a blow to religion as it has been presented for centuries. But are reason and science antithetical to the permeating presence of love that is the mystical essence of God?

Some of us remember the uproar when science and reason had come so far that philosopher Friedrich Nietzsche was moved to write "God is dead." That 1882 statement was widely misunderstood. Nevertheless, the debate about it that flared up in the twentieth century further illustrates how science and reason have eroded creeds and dogmas and how they provide to this day reasons or excuses not to take Christianity seriously.

In the New Christianity Spong sees in John's Gospel, *the statement that there is no God above the sky does not mean that there is no God. Rather, the spiritual presence that permeates the universe can become audible from time to time in a particular person. In this case it was Jesus, but God cannot be confined to the life of Jesus. Jewish mysticism, like mysticism everywhere, could not tolerate any human limits.*

Finally, what about the official's state of mind? What about the choice he made to seek out Jesus, not stealthily like Nicodemus, not by accident like the Samaritan woman. Did he cross the Jew/gentile divide because he had faith in the outcome? Did he "believe" because he was sure that Jesus would heal his son? Neither Spong nor I see faith that way. I find some of his language about faith a bit opaque here, but he does plainly say that *faith gives us only the courage to put one foot in front of the other and walk into tomorrow with integrity even though we know . . . there is no peace of mind, no security, and no safety.*

For me, a clearer statement of the same concept is found in *Active Hope* by Joanna Macy and Chris Johnstone. Choosing the title term rather than "faith," they define it this way:

> Like tai chi or gardening, it is something we do rather than have . . . First, we take a clear view of reality; second, we identify what we hope for . . . third, we take steps to move ourselves or our situation in that direction. Since active hope doesn't require our optimism, we can apply it even in areas where we feel hopeless.

This would appear to accurately describe the mythical official from Capernaum. He may have summoned up the courage to come to Jesus, but it strains credulity that he would have been confident that everything would work out just fine. Notice that neither Spong nor Macy and Johnstone assign any role at all to thinking about outcomes. When we arise each day, we are presented with the power to make choices. That power does not include determining outcomes. It does provide the power to look realistically at our situation, decide what we want, and take actions that are within our control to move things in that direction. That is what the official did. He had faith.

The text of this short story tells us that it is the second sign given by Jesus on his return to Galilee.

The story is a good example of what is there if we only get beyond literalism and understand even a little about mysticism! In this short story, we have seen insight about new ways to look at inclusion, God, and faith. It isn't easy. And it sure wasn't easy for Jewish leaders, or for Jesus, as we will see in another healing story.

CHAPTER 12

The Man Crippled for Thirty-Eight Years

CONTEXT IS IMPORTANT TO the understanding of any text. In addition to being alert to whether accounts and characters are intended to be taken literally, attention must be paid to the political, religious, and economic setting that produced them. This is particularly important for us here. We are trying to grasp how to read John's stories with the eyes of a Jewish mystic. By now we have seen that this involves accepting nearly every protagonist as a literary invention. What then are we to make of the real-life context of these fictional accounts? Is it relevant?

This is a particularly brilliant story in part because it presents for us choices that are even more stark than those faced by Nicodemus, the Samaritan woman, and the gentile official. Like those three, the unnamed cripple was offered a "new consciousness," a term Spong uses often. Be all that as it may, the story of the fictional cripple was produced at a time when its authors faced a real-world threat from Jewish religious leaders. Keep both the spiritual and human dimensions in mind as the story unfolds.

It is no surprise that the writers have Jesus again visiting Jerusalem, the center of Judaic authority, during a religious festival. There he encounters the unnamed cripple at a pool. Popular legend had it that when the water was disturbed, the first person to enter the pool after the disturbance subsided would be cured of any ailment.

Jesus, we are told, knew that the man had been ill for a long time. He asked the man if he wished to be well again. Now one might think that the answer would be what many call today a "no-brainer." "Of course I want to be cured. What a dumb question. By the way, who are you?" Of course, the man's answer expresses his desire to be cured. But his wish is enfolded in an excuse. His response is to complain that there is never anyone there to carry him to the water when it begins to be disturbed. By the time he can get himself there, someone else has been first to go in.

Being restored to physical wholeness after many years would be a life changing event, to say the least. It would take courage and commitment to truly desire such a radical change and find a way to bring it about. It was much easier for the man to say that he really wanted to change, but the reason he could not was always someone else's fault, or just his bad luck.

Jesus did not accept this invitation to argue about the man's excuse. He simply told the man to pick up his sleeping mat and walk. The man did so. He was immediately cured.

This time, it was certainly not the man's faith that gave him physical healing. We see this clearly from his role in the second part of the story. We are told that the incident occurred on the Sabbath. The man is confronted by Jewish leaders, who inform him that he has violated a Sabbath rule by working on that day. Apparently, it was the act of a healthy man carrying a sleeping pallet that constituted the violation. Not exactly the crime of the century but still serious business in the context of Jewish society in Jerusalem. The Sabbath rules are derived from nothing less than what we call the Ten Commandments. In remembrance that God rested on the seventh day in the Genesis creation story, the statement is "remember the Sabbath Day and keep it holy."

There are other more often cited examples of Jesus dealing with this petty type of violation. The writers of Matthew and Luke, for example, wrote of Jesus responding to the authorities when his disciples were sampling a few ears of corn as they walked through a cornfield on the Sabbath. In the other three Gospels, Jesus made it quite clear that doing good works on the Sabbath is not forbidden. "The Sabbath belongs to man, not man to the Sabbath." He also made it clear that the authorities were not the ones truly in charge of Sabbath observance.

The story of the crippled man at the pool is not even included in most commentary about the Bible stories of working on the Sabbath. But my rational legal mind sees an even more nuanced spiritual dimension there.

For example, defining the acts of Jesus' disciples picking a few ears of corn as a violation of the Sabbath work ban is obviously petty. That is apparent to almost anyone. But seen as a general matter of policy, enacting a work ban on the Sabbath is a perfectly legitimate way to honour God by following an ancient commandment. And in fact, one would be surprised if picking corn were not included under such a ban. It is not that the rule has no understandable policy purpose that makes it ridiculous. Rather, the fault lies in how those in charge of making the general rule operational have lost track of any rational underpinning for it. We have many examples of that today.

In the story of the cripple at the pool, Jewish authorities had not only uncoupled their rules from policy but from all rationality. A newly healed person is working when he carries his sleeping pallet?

Remember that these were the same leaders who were fashioning and interpreting rules that presented obstacles to those who wanted to be Jewish Christians. At this time, the religious powers that be had become greatly enamored of themselves and their power to prescribe the only acceptable ways to honor God. They debated one another and took pride in fashioning ever-more-nitpicking versions of the rules for doing that.

So these proclivities of the Jewish leaders were part of the context of both the fictional story of the cripple at the pool and the real situation faced by the writers of John. Christianity was arising from Judaism. Traditional Jews followed an ever more intricate set of rules fashioned during exile in Babylon, defined and dictated by the current leadership. What was to be required of one who wished to be a Jewish Christian? Would different requirements apply to a gentile who simply wished to become a member of the Christian community?

It is not difficult to understand that in this context a real hostility developed between leaders of traditional Judaism and those who wanted to be both Christians and Jews and to be part of a religious community that welcomed gentiles as well. This conflict escalated until the Johannine Christians were expelled from the synagogue around 88 CE.

It was in the midst of this real-world conflict that the story of the cripple at the pool was written and the authors made the Jewish rule makers look even more ridiculous and even more sinister than had the earlier Gospel writers. Not even the strained logic of calling the picking of a few ears of corn unlawful would work to justify the ridiculous charge leveled against the newly healed pool visitor. The law against working on

THE MAN CRIPPLED FOR THIRTY-EIGHT YEARS

the Sabbath, interpreted this way, was just a comment on the arrogance of the Jewish leaders.

Returning to the story of the now-healed cripple, we see that he had learned little or nothing from his amazing experience. When accused, he fell back on excuses. He told them he was not responsible. He was just following orders. "The one who healed me said to me, 'Take up your pallet and walk.'"

Perhaps sensing an opportunity to catch a higher-up, the authorities pressed for the identity of the one who gave the order. We are now truly in the realm of the absurd, looking to round up everyone involved in the big pallet-carrying caper.

Our former cripple had to answer honestly that he did not know who gave him the command that worked so well. But the authors of John could not let the story end there. Jewish leaders were going to ridiculous lengths to claim exclusive prescriptive power in all things related to the relationship between humans and God. That could not go unchallenged. If it did, the real-life story of the nascent Christian community and its very different vision of God would be mortally threatened. Jesus had to reappear in the story. He does.

We have seen several ways that Spong's reading of John challenges standard Christianity. We have seen, for example, that Christianity's "founding fathers" could not abide the radical inclusion that John saw Jesus bringing. Accepting that would diminish their ability to limit the human experience with God to their prescribed rules, in the same way the Jewish leaders were doing in the story. As the story continues, Jesus deals an even greater blow to both orthodoxies.

Jesus finds the man in the temple and gives him one more chance to see beyond physical healing, to grasp the opportunity for life that he has been offered. Unable to do this, the man then rats Jesus out to the Jewish authorities.

The ensuing confrontation between Jesus and the Jewish leadership reveals another component of New Christianity. It also confirms that the authorities were onto a much bigger crime. Jesus told them that his father works on the Sabbath and so does he. Horrors! Blasphemy! Now the man implies that he is God's equal!

Jesus here undermines a very basic element of orthodoxy. He introduces the element of oneness. Jesus asserts his oneness with God and his offer of that oneness to everyone. As Spong sees it, *the one who believes this does not fall under judgment but has passed from death into life, from a limited consciousness to a participation in the universal consciousness that transcends every human limit and every boundary, even the boundary that separates us from eternal life.*

In his response to the Jewish leaders, Jesus speaks of offering eternal life to those who can understand and believe his message. Traditional Christianity sees that as an offer of some wonderful existence after physical death, somewhere up above, to those who will believe that Jesus is one third of God, who came down from up there somewhere to save them from the damnation that otherwise awaits them. Progressive denominations downplay or finesse the scarier parts of this catechism, but it is the basic product on offer.

New Christianity offers something quite different. It offers a spiritually unique individual, born of a woman in the ordinary fashion, with a family that included siblings. Yet one who was aware as no other of every dimension of an infinite and loving God that lived within him and lives within all of us. A God that cannot be controlled. A God who calls us to live beyond what we think are human limits—right now, as well as after our human journey ends. That is the mystical part. How do we live today beyond the guidance that our reason provides? How do we transcend human limits?

In the Unity Movement, a similar Christian path, Jesus is seen not as Savior but as the ultimate Way-Shower. I think that characterization would have resonated with Spong and the writers of John.

We can go beyond literalism and recognize the value of myth and allegory. And there is much there for us when we do. The sin, sacrifice, and salvation interpretation of the Gospels can rationally be drawn out by going that far. But what if we can go even further?

The story of the cripple at the pool revealed one core aspect of a New Christianity. If Jesus is one with God and we can be also—here and now—then religious authorities have no ability to control God—or us. Little wonder that we are told in the story that this is the point where Jewish leaders began plotting to kill Jesus. Little wonder that even the most progressive Christian denominations today politely tuck Spong's New Christianity away in the "liberal theologian" pigeonhole and hope nobody makes too much of it.

We cannot end our consideration of this story without offering a sad farewell to the man at the pool. He may well represent a segment of Jews who wanted to be part of this radical new cult called Christianity while somehow retaining their Jewishness. He was given a spectacular invitation to be part of a transformative life, one that would affect him in ways far more significant than the ability to walk. A new and different wholeness.

But unlike the Samaritan woman and the gentile official, he could not appreciate what he had experienced. He could not even consider going beyond human limits. Like Nicodemus, a man of high learning, this member of the lower social order also had to retreat to the comfort and security of being told what to do. In return for that security, they both ceded much to the rule makers.

Like many of today's intellectuals, Nicodemus knew intuitively that there was something more. His Judaism was not meeting his life needs. We are not told anything about the background of the man at the pool. But his invitation surely came in far more startling form than that of Nicodemus. Why did he not, in a far different manner and for a far different purpose, ask the same questions posed to Jesus by the Jewish leaders? In today's society, who could he represent?

Perhaps the man at the pool would have had a better chance to be alert to the real miracle being offered him if he had been part of the multitude of his peers described in the next two stories, the fourth and fifth signs.

CHAPTER 13

Andrew and Philip

The Red Sea and Manna

This is one of the most powerful chapters in the book. The story of the feeding of the multitude is the fourth sign. The fifth is the other seemingly miraculous event of the day, the contemporaneous account of Jesus walking on water.

These stories are linked in the chapter to demonstrate unmistakably to the Jews that Jesus is the one spoken of by Moses and the prophets. They are also signs to gentiles, i.e., anyone on the planet not a Jew, that what Jesus offers is also available to them. I note, however, that there is no claim that Jesus is the only person selected by God to open the door that he is opening. There have been other spiritual leaders in other cultures at other times with a similar message and purpose. Their status is a subject beyond the scope of this work. From the entire Jesus story, however, I conclude that imperial exclusivism in Christian missionary work is probably misguided. Better to make an effort to understand and respect all faith traditions and not try to confine the work of God to a particular time, place or theology. Again, I think Spong would agree: Many paths. One God. The path offered by Jesus should be offered, not insisted upon or imposed.

I also find compelling the clear contention that these signs are best understood not literally, or even solely as metaphor or allegory, but mystically.

The impact of these stories is highlighted by a variation in John's choice of characters to illustrate them. Instead of the purely literary creations used to reveal earlier signs, e.g. the gentile officer's son, the man crippled thirty-eight years, the authors use obscure disciples Andrew and Philip to link the fourth and fifth signs and show that Jesus really is the Messiah foretold by Moses and the prophets.

The authors of the Synoptics do little more than name Andrew and Philip. John gives them stories, distinct personalities. Indeed, John develops and connects the two signs through them. In chapter 1, John identifies Andrew, brother of Simon Peter, and Philip as the first disciples called. From the outset both are said to understand that Jesus is the Messiah. They also seem to understand that they are to spread the word. Philip goes straight away to tell a man called Nathaniel. But, like so many of us, the two disciples are to find that claiming a belief is quite a different thing from recognizing how it plays out in life.

Once again, Spong warns that these stories are not descriptions of real events that happened in real time. To read them that way is to misread John's intention. Instead, he explains that the sense of the stories can be grasped first by understanding the meaning attributed to Andrew and Philip, and finally what the stories would mean in the Hebrew tradition that made them understandable to the followers of Jesus.

I add here one further observation. I cannot attribute it to Spong, though I suspect he might agree with me. I have noted that what Jesus offered would be available to the whole world, while observing that he did not claim to be the only figure in all of human history to open that door. Would these signs have any meaning for gentiles?

Gentiles were unmistakably part of the multitude in these stories. Without elaborating, Spong points out that in the seminal work of Mark, as well as in Matthew there are two versions of the stories, one taking place on the Jewish side of the lake and a slightly different version taking place on the gentile side.

Spong also speculates that John's motives in developing the story through Andrew and Philip might have something to do with the fact that they are the two disciples with Greek, not Hebrew, names. And throughout the New Testament, of course, we see the assertion that the good news is to be taken "first to the Jew, then to the gentile." We are left in these stories with the question of what, if anything, the gathered gentiles would have made of the fourth and fifth signs. But clearly they were not to be excluded from this teaching.

There is further evidence of the universality to be found in the stories. It is important to remember that these signs come at a time when Jesus is not only offering a new vision of Christianity; he is offering it to a new community of Christians: *By the time John wrote, Jesus' disciples had been cast out of the synagogue. So John was saying to them that Jesus must be to them both a new Moses and a new doorway into the meaning of God . . .*

As the stories unfold, Andrew and Philip are the principal characters in the feeding of the multitude. Even though we have been told in chapter 1 that both disciples grasp that Jesus is the Messiah, neither seems to have their mind on that here.

Jesus opens the conversation by testing Philip's understanding of the implications of what he is supposed to know. Assuming that he is responsible for feeding the people, Jesus asks where they can get bread. Philip's response reflects again the disappointing literalism to which so many of us are prone. He does not see that the subject is a different kind of bread. He responds that buying the bread won't work because two hundred denarii would buy only a fraction of what is needed.

Andrew doesn't get it either, but he is a bit closer to understanding how spirit manifests in daily life. He points out that there is a boy present who has five barley loaves and two fish. It is Spong's view that Andrew is under no illusion that this will solve the problem. But he thinks of the always-deferential Andrew as the patron saint of ordinary people. Accordingly, Andrew thinks there is nothing too small or insignificant to be used and even valued.

So the stage is set. The symbolic meal is served.

Andrew's gesture reminds us that even though this Gospel is meant to be understood mystically, there is also value in finding metaphor and allegory in the stories as well. This truth is part of the enhanced value of all the Bible stories. Letting go of literalism can enhance rather than diminish these sacred texts.

For example, one could imagine that Andrew's gesture of offering the boy's loaves and fishes perhaps triggered a great wave of sharing, a renewed sense of community among the multitude, Jew and gentile alike. Inclusion. After all, it is reasonable to assume that some would have brought food to the event, while others did not.

That would be a valuable symbolic meaning to ascribe to the story, but the authors of John had an even greater lesson in mind. Remember, this gathering was a teaching event. The loaves and fishes were distributed to "those who were ready," and if we are indeed speaking here of teaching about the bread of life, there was even more for people to learn. When those who were ready had had their fill, there was a significant amount left unconsumed.

The multitude, including Jews and gentiles, continues to play an important role as the story of the fifth sign unfolds. Here the Gospel reports a vignette about which I am somewhat surprised that Spong makes no comment.

After the meal, Jesus escaped alone into the hills because he saw that the people were coming to take him by force and make him king. His was a powerful rejection of an institution that was fundamental in the lives of Jew and gentile alike, though particularly for Jews. Centuries earlier, they had demanded an end to the era of governance by judges and insisted upon a religious king. Before and after their Babylonian captivity in the hands of a foreign king, they had experienced all manner of kings: benevolent kings, religious reformers, corrupt kings. Kings were influential in every aspect of life. Who knows what might have transpired if Jesus had encouraged the multitude?

His extraordinary rejection of a nascent movement to make him king in this story is even more remarkable when seen in the context of the story's ensuing revelations that he is the one about whom Moses and the prophets spoke. The most revered Jewish king was David. Gospel writers Matthew and Luke, followed by church authorities for centuries, strove to persuade Christians that acknowledging Jesus as Messiah must include recognition of his status as descendant of that revered king. Invention of the lovely fictional Christmas stories that move his birth from Nazareth to Bethlehem, the city of David, is but one small example of this effort.

If, as Spong contends and I accept, Jesus is opening a door to a new consciousness, a new doorway into the meaning of God, a new way to have life more abundantly now, then this definitive act of rejecting the accepted path to power has to be viewed as highly significant. Elsewhere, Jesus would use language people could understand to teach them that the "kingdom" of God was now. But that kingdom would be unlike anything they or their ancestors had ever experienced.

So, this one sentence account is quite important. Giving any appearance of approval to a mass movement to make him a ruler in the accepted sense could have been devastating to the new way Jesus was teaching. It also had the potential to bring down violent reprisal from Rome. Indeed, according to Bible historian Bart Ehrman, it was the Roman authorities' perception of kingship claims as political crimes that prompted them to permit the execution of Jesus. This, though Jesus never claimed to be king of the Jews at all.

When Jesus escaped to the hills to avoid those who would make him king, he even fled from the disciples, thus setting the stage for the fifth sign—rejoining them by walking on water.

These signs would remind readers of the two most powerful Moses stories: the parting of the Red Sea to permit escape from Egypt and the feeding of the hungry in the desert with manna.

Jesus, the prophet anticipated by Moses, is now revealed to possess the power that the God of Moses possessed. He can feed the hungry multitude in the wilderness with bread. He can transcend the barrier that water brings when it must be navigated.

Jesus does not split the water. He walks on it, above it. He greets the fearful disciples with the Hebrew name ascribed to God: "I AM. Do not be afraid."

Meanwhile, the adoring multitude is nothing if not persistent. The people continue to seek out Jesus and catch up with him the next day. Jesus then seeks to teach them the difference between manna and what they had been offered the day before. It is here also that what Jesus tries to convey requires of them an understanding of the mystical.

The people are quite attentive, at first asking for evidence of his status but soon asking, "What must we do if we are to do the works that God wants?"

Jesus speaks of the difference between perishable manna and the true bread which gives life to the world. He tells them that he is this bread of life and those who consume it will never be hungry. The people respond, "Sir, give us that bread always."

As the lesson continues, Jesus uses a phrase that we will later see is quite important to understanding New Christianity. Jesus says it is God's will that he lose nothing of what God has given him and that he should "raise it up on the last day." Three more times he makes this promise when describing those who understand and believe in him: "I will raise him up on the last day."

Here is why this phrase may be significant. Standard Christian doctrine has the "last day" happening sometime in the unknown future, after Jesus has been physically resurrected and ascended into "heaven," with his mission of dying to save us from our sins accomplished. That is an understandable interpretation of the Jesus story. But it is not the only plausible one. We will later consider in detail the contention that the glory of Jesus came when he was "raised up" on the cross, and not in the misinterpreted resurrection stories.

Returning to the discourse with the multitude, we see Jesus, as he had with Nicodemus and other characters, explain that he is offering something greater than just a new religion. He is the doorway into the meaning of God. He is the love of God. He is calling on them to abandon the comfort and security of standard religion and enter a new understanding of what it means to be human.

Jesus said he was one with God. How then, could the people be one with him? How could they not only experience a radically new here and now, but continue on in that unity to eternal life, unbound by human limitations? He answered those questions also.

Here those who claim the literal historical accuracy of every word in their particular Bible probably have to head for the exits. The venue of the story changes to the synagogue in Capernaum, and Jesus continues with a startling statement. John has Jesus say that in order for people to take Jesus into their lives, to experience the new consciousness, to partake of the bread of life, they must eat his flesh and drink his blood!

He is quite clear. Anyone who does not eat his flesh and drink his blood will not have the life of which he spoke. But anyone who does will be "raised up" on the last day.

It is not only the literalists who have had trouble with this. Standard Christianity hardly knew what to do with it either. The enigma certainly appeared as part of the familiar ritual of the Eucharist. Some early Christian writers, including Justin the Martyr (circa 150 CE) and fourth-century figures including Augustine argued for something called "transubstantiation." When consecrated, the substance of the bread and wine actually becomes the body and blood of Christ. Only the appearance of bread and wine remains. The Catholic Church affirmed transubstantiation in 1215.

This was serious stuff. In 1539, the English Parliament decreed the death penalty for anyone who denied transubstantiation. The offender was to be burned, without opportunity to recant.

The Protestant Reformation, led by Lutherans, came to feature a variation called "consubstantiation." Here the substance of the bread and wine sort of coexist side-by-side with the body and blood of Christ.

Anglicans, for example, say that the bread and wine contain Jesus' spiritual presence but do not literally transform into body and blood.

Many Protestant denominations today just finesse the whole matter. The ritual is an "ordinance," not a "sacrament," and is observed yearly rather than weekly or daily.

The entire Eucharist, however, has been enlisted in service of the sin, sacrifice, and salvation narrative. The Anglican ritual is typical:

> All glory be to thee, Almighty God, our heavenly Father, for that thou of thy tender mercy didst give thine only Son Jesus Christ to suffer death upon the cross for our redemption; who made there by his one oblation of himself once offered, a full, perfect and sufficient sacrifice, oblation and satisfaction, for the sins of the whole world; and did institute, and in his holy Gospel command us to continue, a perpetual memory of that his precious death and sacrifice, until his coming again.

Spong's understanding is less complicated: *Eat my flesh—take my life into yours. Drink my blood—open your spirit to my spirit. Receive me from the water into your boat.* New doors are being opened. All members of John's early Christian community, including those recently expelled from the synagogue, are being offered something that does not require a synagogue or Torah.

If the real Jesus story is fulfillment, calling for an end to both the authority and the comforting security of the Law and the Prophets, of doctrine and Jewish ritual, what reason is there simply to transition into a Christian model of authority and security, of doctrine and ritual?

For example, New Christianity challenges one of the unfortunate doctrines related to today's Eucharist. The doctrine arose from the fourth century CE Council of Nicaea. The matter featured a spirited dispute over the identity and divinity of Jesus. A church official named Arius insisted that Jesus was a human being who had been promoted by God to divine status. Another theologian, Athanasius, argued that Jesus was divine in the same way as God the Father, "of one substance." Unfortunately, in my view, Athanasius won out. The standard misunderstanding of the preamble to John's Gospel that we have seen has been adopted as a component of his view.

What emerged from the Council of Nicaea was the Catholic and Catholic-derivative Nicene Creed. Worshipers now recite that Jesus was of one being with God, begotten not made; that he came down from heaven to save us and was made man, born of the Virgin Mary; he was crucified but rose again; he ascended back into heaven, but he will return to judge both the living and the dead. The creed goes on to recite fealty to "one holy catholic and apostolic church."

The creed also describes an awkward kind of trinity. God is really three persons: Father, Son, and Holy Spirit. Given the vehement insistence on its monotheism, which one sees in the history of Judaism, and the concurrence by standard Christianity, this arrangement of three equal deities seems a bit strange.

The image we have examined of Jesus inviting us to become part of him as he is part of God suggests a different kind of trinity: One with God. One with Christ. One with one another. Indeed, that seems more consistent with the two New Testament commandments: Love God. Love neighbor as self. Everyone is a neighbor.

I have included a generous number of my own comments here. Spong might not agree with all of them. But I view this as a particularly important chapter. First, because the Gospels do not include many examples of direct teachings ascribed to Jesus as opposed to lessons to be derived from parables and stories of encounters with individuals. Second, because I see in the chapter the outline of Spong's New Christianity emerging more clearly. The doorway to a mystical union with Jesus is also a doorway to understanding a new consciousness of our own divinity and that of others, as well as our relationship to both Jesus and God. It is a story that differs radically from the standard narrative.

In addition to a different nature and mission for Jesus, we have already seen differences involving oneness, radical inclusion, and universality. There is much more.

In the next chapter, featured characters are not disciples like Andrew and Philip but rather the brothers of Jesus. The chapter begins to illuminate further the cast-out early Christian community's split from Judaism.

CHAPTER 14

The Brothers of Jesus

A Debate on Origins

HERE WE FIND THE beginning of the split with Judaism about the nature and mission of Jesus. We will see that the very human Jesus is not simply the fulfillment of the Law and Prophets. He has been chosen by God to be much more than that. This was something that even early Christians were slow to grasp and Jewish officials considered a mortal threat.

The split had to come. If the Law had indeed been fulfilled, it had ended. There must now be something new. But what? Imagine how difficult it would have been for the early Christian communities, steeped in traditional Judaism, to answer that question. It is not surprising that they began to search for what they did not understand by wrapping it in what they did understand. The first step was to establish that Jesus was indeed the Messiah. The next, more complicated step was to understand the Messiah's new message. For this, the story of mystical signs employed by the authors of John differs from that of the other Gospel writers.

The split was real, but so was the close relationship to Jewish lore. Long before the similar work of second- and third-century Christian officialdom, early Christians strove to portray Jesus as the Messiah, the one of whom Moses and the prophets spoke. They transformed Jewish ritual and tradition into messianic settings featuring Jesus whenever possible.

Accordingly, the authors of John set the events of chapters 7 and 8 during Sukkoth, Jewish Thanksgiving. Many customs from that festival mirror the later accounts of Palm Sunday. They include marching with palm fronds and recitation of Ps 118. Among other hints proffered as predictions of the coming of Jesus, for example, the psalm contains what became a bedrock Christian concept: "The stone which the builders rejected has become the chief cornerstone."

This effort at spiritual linkage is another reminder that we are not reading history but rather a non-literal portrait of Jesus.

The story opens with Jesus still in Galilee because Jewish officials in Judea were out to kill him. His brothers urge him to leave and go to Jerusalem, arguing that his works will gather a bigger audience there.

Yes, according to the earliest Christian writings human Jesus had human brothers.

Ironically, those who denied this literal account resorted themselves to literary devices. Their effort was to depict Mary as a perpetual virgin. For example, though now generally discredited, a document called the Protoevangelium has Mary betrothed at age twelve to Joseph, an aged widower who already had sons. Another writer even has Joseph over eighty at the time, with four sons and two daughters.

In John's story Jesus responds to his brothers, just as he did at the Cana wedding, by telling them that his time has not yet come. He will not leave. However, just as he had done in Cana, Jesus eventually does what has been asked of him. He goes to the Jerusalem Temple in secret in the middle of Sukkoth and begins to teach.

A very mixed reaction awaits him. Jewish hierarchy are predictably hostile. Among the temple members, however, are those with open minds as well as many skeptics. For everyone, Jesus faces the challenge of conveying a new plane of understanding.

The ensuing exchange among them reveals much: the bankruptcy of rules-based religiosity, whether Jesus is the Messiah—and more. Remember that the writers of John were Jews desperately trying to figure out how following Jesus related to their traditional faith path. We learn much about where they were on that mission from the story of the exchanges in the temple. It had to be challenging. If Jesus was the Messiah who had fulfilled the prophesies, were the 600+ Judaic laws now obsolete? Did followers now have to split from Judaism, or could they somehow continue to be observant Jews? Either way, how could they fully understand who Jesus was and what he was about?

Jesus illustrates the misplaced priorities of some of his listeners by asking why they were angry with him for making a man whole on the Sabbath when by contrast the law did not forbid circumcision on the Sabbath. He admonished them to support doing what was right rather than concentrating on appearances.

Spong reminds us that they did not grasp this teaching. *They do not yet embrace that his meaning has little to with religion; rather it is about life.*

Some of the members note that the man the authorities want to kill is present and speaking freely. They speculate that perhaps even the chief priests and elders concede that he is the Christ. That speculation moves the story to discussion of another issue of his relation to Judaism. The same one the early Christians were working on. Was Jesus the Judaic Messiah? Unfortunately, the dialogue then begins to deteriorate to questions about the scriptural origin and residency requirements for the Messiah. Jesus did not qualify.

The questioning is reminiscent of the quick judgments we still make about people based on perceived differences. When we ask, "Where are you from?," the response "Alabama" immediately invokes a much different stereotype than "New York." The members knew Jesus was "from" Galilee, while the Messiah had to hail from Bethlehem. Not only that—he had to be descended from David.

Jesus redirects the conversation. He explains that he did not come; he was sent by one that he knows but they do not. This prompts the chief priests and Pharisees to send for the police to arrest him. The police, however, refuse. They must have been listening. They tell the Pharisees, "There has never been anyone who has spoken like this." This may be one occasion when there appears to be some protective force behind the fact that Jesus' "time has not yet come."

On the last day of the festival Jesus returns. He seeks to describe his mission in scriptural terms that are related to the festival and refers again to the kind of water that the Samaritan woman came to understand: "If any man is thirsty, let him come to me! Let the man come and drink who believes in me." Water was an important subject at Sukkoth. There were prayers for rain and ceremonies commemorating the Mosaic water miracle. There were also readings from prophets Zecharia and Ezekiel foretelling life-giving water for Zion.

Jesus is affirming the continuing relevance of Judaism but offering a radical new vision that goes even beyond fulfillment of prophecy. In Jewish thought, water is a synonym for a Holy Spirit.

He tells the crowd that he will only be with them a little longer and where he is going they cannot go. This prompts speculation about whether he will seek to escape beyond the lands under Jewish control. Considering the signs related so far in this Gospel, he was likely again speaking about breaking down every barrier that divides one human being from another.

Some listeners even speculate further that the admonition that they cannot go where he is going means that he is contemplating suicide. Spong sees them as trapped in their self-conscious humanity and unable to see that *Jesus is a doorway into a universal consciousness that no one can know until he or she steps into it.*

The teaching continues, as does the mixed reaction. Jesus says repeatedly that everything he has learned, everything he has done, everything he is, is not of himself but of God. He is not exactly claiming here to be "God in three persons."

Using again the oft-repeated phrase that Spong sees as a reference to the crucifixion, the writers of John have Jesus explain, "When you have lifted up the Son of Man, then you will know that I am He and that I do nothing of myself. What the Father has taught me is what I preach."

At this point, whatever their level of understanding, we are told that "many came to believe in him."

Some of the members seem convinced. Others remain hostile, still maintaining that Jesus cannot pass the "where you from?" test. When Jesus urges them to learn the truth from him and tells them that the truth will set them free, the authorities weigh in. They self-righteously claim that, as descendants of Abraham, they are already free and have never been in bondage.

After reminding them a bit about their history in Egypt, Jesus furthers the split with standard Judaism. He tells the authorities that their claims are not rooted in their status as descendants of Abraham because they do not have the courage to do what Abraham did. Abraham was a risk-taker. He left the security of the world he knew. He went beyond the certainty of religion to experience an expanding faith.

Jesus concludes this deconstruction of official Judaism with the assertion that Abraham would be glad to see Jesus' coming. Further, he reminds them of the preeminence of spirit over religion by invoking again the name given to God in Exodus: "Before Abraham was, I AM." Jesus was claiming to be part of the life of God, of the love of God, of the being of God. It is an experience that can be shared by anyone who walks through the doorway to a new consciousness that he was opening.

But this was too much. As Spong puts it, *those who believe they alone possess "the truth" have to destroy anyone who attacks their religious security*. The people pick up stones to throw at him, but Jesus again escapes. His time had not yet come.

With the interment of standard Judaism begun, early Christians now have answers to some of the questions that troubled them. Standard Judaism was over. Something new and better with meaning for this life was available from Jesus if they could only listen to him in a new way.

This episode could, of course, be interpreted to fit the later narrative of standard Christianity. That narrative, however, is suspect if for no other reason than it is part of a standard Christianity with disturbing similarities to the standard Judaism that Jesus was attacking. Like the God visualized in Judaism, the God of standard Christianity threatens punishment to those who do not worship the exclusive deity properly but offers salvation and glory to those who repent.

As the Fourth Gospel continues, further details of an alternative narrative appear.

That narrative is not consistent with what standard Christianity and its officialdom would construct over the next two centuries.

The next chapter further reveals a view of John's authors that Christianity flows from Judaism but is not a mere continuation of it in an altered form.

CHAPTER 15

The Man Born Blind

The Split from Judaism Is Complete

THIS STORY CAN BE read and understood at the level of allegory or indeed any level except literally. It details the split between Jewish officialdom and the Johannine Christians. Their final exclusion left them with difficult choices to make. But the story also reveals more of what Jesus was offering to those who chose to embrace his message. The symbolism again applies to both the story set in Jesus' time, and to the time this Gospel was written some sixty to sixty-five years later.

Using again the light/darkness theme, John tells the story of what faced the new Christians at this time as if it had happened in the life of "the man born blind."

At the time of the Gospel-writing, Jewish synagogue leaders were taking a hard line. They expelled followers of John from the synagogue and fiercely defended orthodoxy.

What were the new Christians to do now? Steeped in Judaism, they had been blind from birth. The temple had been destroyed in 70 CE. Now they had been declared non-Jews and cast out of the synagogue. Their final exclusion left them with difficult choices to make. Fortunately, the story also reveals more about a new path.

In response to exclusivist expulsion and persecution from religious authorities, some embraced the teaching of Jesus about radical inclusion as part of the kingdom of here and now. They described themselves as the new Israel and went forward to build a faith community that transcended all limits and included women, Samaritans, and gentiles.

But many could not make the transition. The security of the limits that bound the faith of their ancestors was too powerful. They remained in darkness.

There is a similar conflict among characters in the story. It begins with a reminder that even the disciples were subject to the hold of tradition. They ask Jesus, "Who is to blame for the man having been born blind?" Throughout their study of Judaism, they would have accepted the teaching that pain and tragedy are instruments of divine punishment. Blame had to rest with someone. This concept appears often in what we call the Old Testament. Unfortunately, it is also alive and well today in many Christian communities and apparent in the government policies they influence.

But this fellow was born blind. How could he be to blame? The disciples turn to another ingrained teaching of Judaism that has God punishing people for the sins of their parents! Maybe that's it! God sometimes even goes back a few generations to find justification for punishment.

Whatever brought this vision of a God with no sense of fairness or justice to Judaism, it is not a portrait of a God of love whose purpose is to enhance life. To have been taught to identify with such a God from birth was to be blind from birth, to identify God with darkness.

Jesus, of course, tells them that neither the man nor his parents are at fault. Instead, the affliction can be used to bring about a new understanding of God and what human life can be. Adopting again the name ascribed to God, "I AM," Jesus says, "I am the light of the world." It is the old Israel that is now also portrayed as the man who was born blind.

In the story, Jesus heals the man but in a way that serves as a reminder that understanding of a new way seldom comes all at once. Entering new realities usually requires some work from us. The healing of the man's blindness is not instantaneous. (Nor was it in a similar story found in Mark.) In John's story, Jesus mixes spittle with clay, rubs it on the blind man's eyes, and tells him to wash in the pool at Siloam. Only then is his sight restored.

The depth of the blindness of Jewish officials, and their persistent opposition to light continues the story. The formerly blind man's neighbors take him to the Pharisees for interrogation.

In an approach that suggests a degree of desperation, the Pharisees begin by suggesting that maybe the person healed was not really the blind beggar but someone who resembled him. The man stubbornly insists that he is the one who was blind and can now see.

The questioners then turn to the now familiar argument that the healing could not have been of God since Jesus did it on the Sabbath. Jesus must be the sinner! But others present see the holes in this argument. "If it was not of God, how did he manage to do this wonderous thing?"

Having no answer for that, the officials return to the interrogation, asking the man how he views Jesus. He answers that he believes Jesus to be a prophet.

At this point, those whom Spong terms "gendarmes of religious purity" know they certainly cannot leave the matter there. They begin to interrogate the man's parents. But the parents are no help. They confirm that this was their son; he was born blind; they have no idea how he regained his sight. Have to ask him about that.

We are told here that the parents were answering cautiously out of fear of the authorities. Perhaps having this in the story was another example of time shifting. At the time of the Gospel-writing, such a fear was justified. The Jewish officials not only drove the followers of John from the synagogue; they also excluded any others who spoke of Jesus as the Christ whether or not they were part of John's faith community.

Now thoroughly frustrated, the authorities go back to interrogating the man born blind. They ask him about Jesus being the sinner because the healing was done on the Sabbath. The man answers that he doesn't know about that. All he knows is that he was blind and now he can see.

The questioners then resort to an interrogation tactic that is familiar to anyone conversant with the criminal justice system today: have the suspect tell his story over and over until some inconsistency arises. Go from there. "Tell us again how he did it," they ask.

But the man thwarts this effort brilliantly. Reminding them that he has told this story once and they didn't believe him, he asks why they want to hear it again. Perhaps facetiously, he then asks whether it is because they want to become disciples of Jesus? I imagine this was about the last thing the frustrated Pharisees expected to hear from a blind beggar. After one more lame attempt to go back to the argument about Jesus' origin that we saw in the last chapter, they again descend into vitriol and personal attacks on the poor man.

The Gospel writers do not end the story there. They continue the blending of their own expulsion into the literary portrait they have set decades earlier. Jesus goes to find the formerly blind man who has also by now been expelled from the synagogue, cut off from the religion of his birth. At the conclusion of a gentle conversation the man comes to believe and sees that God is present in the life of Jesus.

The story closes with Jesus explaining more about who he is and what he offers the world. Jesus does not mince words. This is the final denunciation of official Judaism. The religious leaders were born blind. That is not, of course, the source of their guilt or of that of the man born blind. Their guilt lies in claiming to see when they do not see. It lies in making a virtue of closed minds. It lies in insisting that the truth of God had been captured in the religious forms of the past.

In Spong's words, it was *to refuse to step into the new life being offered, the new consciousness . . . and new understanding of what life is all about . . . to step beyond human limits into the universal consciousness that Jesus opens the way for all to see and enter.*

In a very real sense, this chapter has been about exclusion and inclusion and about Jesus as a Way-Shower rather than a Savior, as traditionally understood. That is why I was somewhat surprised that Spong chose in the final paragraph to refer only incompletely to a later verse in the Gospel, John 14:6, that has often been used to foster exclusion and exclusivism.

He writes that the claim of Jesus to be "the way, the truth, and the life" means that he is offering the pathway into a divinity that can be found in the expansion and transcendence of human limits.

That is a commendable interpretation of the verse because it focuses on the way Jesus is showing, rather than who he is. The path to the transcendent universal consciousness, to love, to going beyond human limits should be the focal point of understanding here, not any assumed uniqueness of the one who lights the path.

But at this point, Spong does not mention the rest of the verse: "No man comes unto the father but through me." I have had these words thrown in my face more than once as the ultimate proof text that only by accepting sin and salvation Christianity can anyone, anywhere, be "saved." So, I am grateful that Spong's fellow theologian Marcus Borg picks up the thread.

Borg also focuses on the universality of the message, but he addresses the misused part of the verse as well. Examining the metaphor, he points out that "A way is a path or road or a journey, not a set of beliefs . . . Thinking that the only people who can be saved are those who know the word 'Jesus' amounts to salvation by syllables . . . The way of Jesus is not a set of beliefs about Jesus."

Where does the way lead? From start to finish in all the Gospels it leads to Jesus' death. As we will see, for John that is his glorification. But it is the path of dying to an old way of being, and being born into a new way of being, that is being claimed as the only way to God.

Borg recounts a conversation with a Hindu colleague who agreed that this was indeed the meaning of "The Way," and that Jesus is the only way, a universal way known in all the religions of the world. The two agree that the way of Jesus is a way known to millions who have never heard of Jesus.

The last of the signs Spong explains in detail is the story of two literary creations named Lazarus. The story represents a coda on the understandable but tragic narrative we have followed about official Jewry. It is about their inability to consider transcending human limits of security, fear, isolation, suspicion—even in the face of the most wondrous of all works.

CHAPTER 16

Lazarus

Breaking the Final Barrier

It is that wondrous work, bringing back to life one who is unmistakably dead, that draws the Book of Signs to a close and provides the setting for what is termed the farewell discourses. This story could easily be seen as part of the standard sin and salvation narrative, as could many of the others so far. But that is not the way the writers of John intended it to be understood. It is in the relationship between this and the story of a different Lazarus in Luke (16:19–31) that the purpose of John's writers is revealed, as we see after yet another caution against reading literally.

John's Lazarus is a friend of Jesus and the brother of Mary and Martha. As was true with the earlier signs, the stunning event depicted here does not happen instantly. Neither did the final break between John's early Christian community and Judaism. Neither did the arrival for those new Christians of a full understanding about what was happening in their lives.

After hearing the news of Lazarus's death, Jesus waits two days to take the short journey from Jerusalem to Bethany. Both Mary and Martha complain about this, suggesting that if he had come earlier Lazarus might not have died. In this story, there is no doubt that Lazarus is dead. He has been in his grave for four days when Jesus arrives. The corpse is already beginning to decay.

The mix of witnesses to what happens next is important. We are told that a crowd of mourners, Jerusalem Jews, attended to comfort Mary and

Martha. But as with many of the assemblages we have seen, there are some who are eager to believe, some who are skeptical, and some who are hostile.

The event itself would surely have been awe-inspiring. Jesus goes to the tomb. The stone is removed. He calls for Lazarus to come out and, still wrapped in burial cloth, Lazarus obeys. This is not only going beyond turning water to wine by supplying an abundant 150 gallons, beyond healing a crippled man who had been in that condition for thirty-eight years, beyond giving sight to a blind man who had been blind from birth. This has to top all of the "miracle" stories.

Naturally, the story could be read as a foretelling of the death of Jesus and his physical resurrection. That view is found in much of orthodox Christianity and embellished by different accounts of his post-resurrection activity and ascension into heaven. Even a good analogy is not perfect, however, and there are significant problems with this one. Who was Lazarus? Why did he fall ill and die? What did he do after his resurrection? What does he have to do with sin?

It is more likely that Spong is right. This is not a story of a real event, but if seen through Jewish eyes it is quite an important one.

In Luke, there is a story of another Lazarus, who might well have also been a source for John. Understanding their relationship reveals the importance of both.

Luke's Lazarus is a poor beggar at the door of a rich man, Dives [Deyevees]. The rich man sees no value in the life of the likes of Lazarus and curtly leaves him to starve.

When both men die, Lazarus goes to the "bosom of Abraham," depicted as a good place to be. Dives goes to a place of unspeakable torment, which is quite warm. Still viewing Lazarus as a member of the servant class, there to fill his needs, Dives cries out to Abraham to send Lazarus to at least give him a drop of water to ease the anguish of the flames.

Abraham refuses, reminding Dives of the different lives the two had led and pronouncing that justice has been done. Dives then pleads for Abraham to send Lazarus to warn his family so that they could repent and avoid the place of torment. Lazarus, of course, would have to be resurrected for that to happen.

But Abraham again refuses, saying, "If they do not hear Moses and the prophets, neither will they be convinced if someone should rise from the dead." This pronouncement is the link between John's Lazarus and Luke's.

Would the guardians of the religion of Moses and the prophets in John's Lazarus story understand and believe in Jesus and his new purpose and message? By now we know the answer to that. But could others be commissioned?

We are told that some of those who witnessed the raising of Lazarus believed in Jesus. Some, however, not only did not but decided to go straight to the synagogue authorities with the news.

As predicted in Luke's story, the Pharisees were not convinced even by someone rising from the dead. To recognize Jesus as the one of whom Moses and the prophets spoke would mean giving up a great deal of security, as well as power over the religious lives of Jews. At the time of both stories, power over religious lives meant power over all aspects of life. That power derived in significant measure from the enforced isolation from others that was so apparent in the increased control exercised since the return from exile in Babylon. Accepting this Jesus would mean that all of those things that keep members of the human family apart would disappear.

Luke's Lazarus story ends with Abraham's final refusal. John's does not.

In it, this ultimate sign causes synagogue authorities to become even more fearful. They correctly see Jesus as the ultimate threat to their tribal and religious life. They decide that Jesus must die.

In a meeting led by high priest Caiaphas they conclude that Jesus must die for national security reasons. They reason that if they don't kill him the people will follow him and the Romans will put an end to their whole Jewish nation. This was no trivial concern. At the time of both the Gospel writing and that of Jesus, the Jewish hierarchy had made an accommodation with Rome that preserved much of their autonomy. Unfortunately, killing people one does not understand in service of a "higher cause" remains a practice of many in power today.

However, after Caiaphas pronounces that it is better for one man to die than for the whole nation to be destroyed, John's writers add the mystical interpretation that this prophesy was not about Jesus dying "for the nation only, but to gather together in unity the scattered children of God." For them, the life of Jesus, and his death at the insistence of Jewish leadership, spoke of human oneness.

This radical inclusion and radical new awareness, the idea of a new universal consciousness, of actually entering into the eternal life of God, must have been a frightening matter to the Jewish members of the new Christian community. Their religious experience had been steeped in isolation and sacrifice to a jealous God who rewards obedience to a myriad of rules and punishes violators and their families.

To be sure, there are strong social justice admonitions to be found in standard Judaism as well. That is also the true heart of Christianity. But it is understandable that the Christian hierarchy to come would gradually develop a structure similar to that of the Jews, with a similar emphasis on sin, sacrifice, punishment, and salvation, and a similar set of rules they would define and administer. Spong's New Christianity, emerging from his view of John's mystical writing, challenges all that.

The story ends by telling us that from the day of this meeting on, the Jewish leaders were determined to kill Jesus. Demonstrating the arrogance of power, they even issue an order requiring that anyone who knew the whereabouts of Jesus inform them so they could arrest him. Ultimately, they decide to kill Lazarus as well.

Jesus withdraws to a nearby town and spends time with his disciples in preparation for the Passover that would be his last.

Spong does not devote a separate chapter to what follows in the next chapter of John's Gospel. He simply adds a few paragraphs, referring to chapter 12 of the Gospel as a transition to the account of the final discourses. And so it is, but perhaps it deserves a bit more attention.

Six days before the Passover, Jesus returns to the home of Mary and Martha in Bethany. They give a dinner for him, and Lazarus is present. Mary anoints Jesus with her hair, using a costly ointment. Thus, in the presence of the disciples, Jesus is at once made part of a ritual that is to symbolically identify him as the anointed, the chosen one, and also prepare him for death.

Chapter 12 also includes the account of Jesus' triumphal entry into Jerusalem, now celebrated by Christians as Palm Sunday. The story is important once again because of those who observe this and those with whom Jesus speaks on that day.

The crowd includes observant Jews who have come to see Jesus but were also curious to see the new celebrity, Lazarus. The size of the crowd produced more panic from the Pharisees.

Also present is a group of gentile partial converts to Judaism, who worship at certain Jewish festivals. Through the disciples, this group had obtained a meeting with Jesus, and it was to them that he chooses to reveal that "now the hour has come for the Son of Man to be glorified." Yet another example of radical inclusion.

While they are present, a voice comes from heaven assuring Jesus that his name has been glorified and would be glorified again. To the wondering bystanders, Jesus explains that the voice was for their sake, not his. He goes on to state, "And when I am lifted up from the earth, I shall draw all men to myself." John clarifies that this statement was not a reference to going back "up there." Rather, "lifted up from the earth" indicated the kind of death he would die.

Finally, the mixed reaction from practicing Jews continues. Some believe. Some do not. Some leaders believe but hold back for fear of expulsion by the Pharisees.

To all in the gathered public, Jesus explains his identity a final time: "Whoever believes in me believes not in me but in the one who sent me . . . what the Father has told me is what I speak."

The stage is set for the final teachings.

PART III

The Farewell Discourses
and the High Priestly Prayer

CHAPTER 17

Peter and the Commandment to Love

SPONG PREPARES READERS FOR a shift in method and approach as *The Fourth Gospel* turns toward its climax. The focus is now on the disciples, not the public, as they journey with Jesus toward Jerusalem. Once again, the story has the disciples anticipating existential issues very similar to those the community of John was facing sixty-five to seventy years later. Persecution. Separation.

In the story, the disciples are dealing with the fearful question of what they will do when Jesus is no longer with them and how to face the anticipated retribution by Jewish leaders. In this context it makes perfect sense for Jesus to change his method of teaching and speak to them directly. The teaching method described in this Gospel already differed from that found in the Synoptics, e.g., no parables and no short sayings. In John we have learned to this point from stories of Jesus' conversations with a variety of actors, who are the literary creations so important to the Book of Signs. Now we learn from monologues directed at several historical figures.

Jesus speaks directly to the disciples—and to us. It is in Spong's mystical interpretation of the first discourse that we find the heart of his New Christianity.

The farewell discourses are set in the days before Passover. The first is presented at a meal, not a Passover Seder but a fellowship gathering with disciples. The crucifixion is near. The supper is a final opportunity for Jesus to explain the divine love in him, to open the door to all people to this love. As soon as they grasp its meaning, they will experience a new dimension of their existence and purpose.

We see in the discourses that the absolute heart of Jesus' mission and message is love. However, it is a love that differs significantly from the love expounded by standard Christianity. Both Catholic and Protestant traditions, with the hard edges sometimes smoothed to a greater or lesser degree, speak of God loving us enough to send Jesus down to save us sinners from the terrible fate that has been our destiny since the garden of Eden. Why? The fifty-cent words "apocalyptic eschatology" tell us that it is so that believers, whether alive or dead, can join Jesus when he returns and go up to heaven with him.

The more extreme elements of standard Christianity include exclusivism and exclusion as part of this message. The contention is that theirs is the only truth and anyone who doesn't accept it is condemned. To their credit, the more benign elements of standard Christianity downplay, omit, or finesse this troubling dogma. But all are offering the same basic message.

Paul termed the love Jesus is trying to get his followers to understand as *agape*.

Love without limits. Selfless love that changes our present life. Again, Jesus is inviting them to a new dimension of living life in the present.

At this meal, Jesus takes startling action to illustrate his words about love. The focal character in the mythological event is the real person Peter, a figure who would have been familiar to early Christians.

In an account found only in John, Jesus removes his outer clothing, wraps himself in a towel, and begins washing the feet of the disciples and wiping them with the towel. The protective security barriers we rely upon in our associations have been symbolically removed. The accepted status of relationships has been turned on its head.

Jesus, the master teacher that the disciples have been moved to follow, sometimes at great risk to themselves, has assumed the role of servant. Incidentally, this was a far more powerful act than the empty ritual that kings and popes would make centuries later when they would temporarily descend, wash the feet of a selected group of poor people, and then return to their exalted positions.

Like some of us, Peter senses the message here, but he can't quite handle it. He protests, "Lord, you do not wash my feet." He is fearful of being part of a love where there are no master/servant relationships, where the status

PETER AND THE COMMANDMENT TO LOVE

games that people play no longer work, where he might experience a new awareness.

Jesus explains what he has done. And the explanation includes the answer to what his followers are to do when he is gone. He tells them that whoever welcomes him into the new dimension will be welcoming the one who sent him. God is love, and love is not so much an entity as it is an experience. When this love lives in them, they will serve the world.

He tells the disciples that he will not be with them much longer and, as he told the Jewish leaders, where he is going they cannot go. Like Peter, who only partially understands, their awareness is not yet fully developed. There is a path they can walk that will take them to where Jesus is going. It is not a geographical path. Rather, every step of the path will be revealed by living what he terms a new commandment—that they love one another. That is how they will be known as his people. That is how they will serve the world. That is how they will discover their oneness with him, with God, and with one another.

Peter, acting again a lot like us, still doesn't get it. He asks again where Jesus is physically going. Jesus patiently responds that Peter can not come with him now, but he will be able to follow later. Peter is not mollified. Again, as we sometimes do, he petulantly demonstrates that he thinks he knows more than he actually does. Peter says, "Why can't I follow you now? I will lay down my life for you." Christians today know how that story ends—with Jesus correctly predicting that Peter will deny even knowing him.

The commandment Jesus gave was indeed a new one. As noted, it is not the kind of love that is a feature of the sin/sacrifice/atonement message of standard Christianity. Neither is it the kind of love that is an integral part of traditional Judaism.

As the first discourse continues, we learn more in the next chapter about atonement theology, about the identity and purpose of Jesus, and the importance of his death to New Christianity.

CHAPTER 18

Not Atonement but Glory!

John Clarifies Jesus' Death

IN THIS CHAPTER, SPONG challenges one of the foundational assertions underlying standard Christianity and provides insights into an equally foundational assertion of New Christianity. The chapter deals with fundamental questions. What is the significance of the crucifixion? Why did Jesus die? Was his death a sacrifice to God on our behalf to save us miserable sinners from damnation? Was it something else?

Here it becomes somewhat difficult to keep the story simple. I know that the reader's level of knowledge and interest in things biblical varies greatly. As I try my best, I apologize for laying out again parts of the standard narrative with which they are already familiar. I apologize also to the non-religious for the brief trip into the theology of Jewish rituals.

Spong reminds readers at the outset that in the discourses, we are not reading the actual words of Jesus. On the subject of his death, we are reading an interpretation of an experience with Jesus, by a particular set of writers, in a particular community, many years after the crucifixion.

Those writers were Jewish. The Jewish members of the community had already undergone expulsion from the synagogue that had caused some to abandon Christianity and return to traditional Judaism. Later, the community split again over how to understand the relationship between God and Jesus. More Jewish members went back to the religion of their ancestors. But this left the remainder, including the writers of John, free to move to a new understanding of Jesus that included the meaning and significance of his death.

On that issue, we are reminded that both the defectors and the remainder were steeped in Jewish history and rituals. Indeed, this was true of all biblical tellers of the Jesus story, including all the Gospel authors and Paul. The later architects of standard Christianity did not have nearly their degree of such knowledge.

This gap in an understanding of Judaism came to shape an interpretation that would later be called the "doctrine of atonement" in standard Christianity. Spong contends that a better understanding of Judaism might lead to a radically different interpretation, one that is important to a New Christianity.

It was not Spong's purpose to flatly declare the standard story wrong. Nor is it mine. I have already mentioned witnessing some wonderful work by those who accept it. But the alternative, revealed from the same sources, resonates with me and with many. It deserves something approaching equal time. A markedly different vision of the crucifixion is especially important.

In John, unlike the Synoptics, we do not find the "doctrine of atonement." That doctrine portrays Jesus being offered up as a sacrifice to God to save us from the consequences of the sinful acts that humans had continued to commit over the centuries since the first by Adam and Eve.

This interpretation is understandable. All the Gospel writers and their readers were likely familiar with the first written pronouncement about the crucifixion. Connecting Christianity with its Jewish roots, Paul wrote, "He died for our sins in accordance with the Scriptures" (1 Cor 15:3). From that point, atonement theology as I have characterized it here has dominated standard Christianity.

But what did Paul mean? And how were early Christians to connect the death of Jesus to those Scriptures? The standard Christian doctrine of atonement is not the only answer to questions about how Paul could have understood the story or how we should see the meaning of Jesus' death.

Paul was a learned Jew. His primary mission, however, was to gentiles, and it was they who interpreted this pronouncement at the time and over the ensuing centuries. Although they were not completely unfamiliar with Jewish history, the church fathers who produced the doctrine of atonement paid little or no mind to the role of Jewish myth, prophesy, and ritual in shaping the Gospel stories about the death of Jesus. They were mainly interested in interpreting the Old Testament stories and prophesies as a

PART III | THE FAREWELL DISCOURSES

way to prove in detail that Jesus was the Messiah—descended from David, born in Bethlehem, etc. They fit the atonement doctrine into that prophetic transition story. Their ignorance or indifference to the influence of Jewish ritual in the Gospel telling of the crucifixion story, however, masks consideration of a very different meaning for it.

Why do humans construct ceremonies of ritual sacrifice? What are we supposed to learn from that practice?

The Jews of history had more than one ritual having to do with sacrifice. Those rituals offer different answers to these questions. The ceremonies focused the minds of worshipers on different aspects of their relationship with God and its impact on their lives.

Two traditional Jewish rituals, as well as writings found in the book of Isaiah, are important to both standard Christianity and Spong's New Christianity. Seeing the rituals through both Jewish eyes and those of the less informed founders of standard Christianity requires us to start at the beginning—the book of Genesis.

It was upon the Genesis creation stories that late-fourth-century Bishop Augustine and the founding fathers of organized Christianity who followed over the centuries built the doctrine of atonement. Understanding their interpretation of those Genesis stories is necessary to a different understanding of the remainder of the first discourse and the characters employed in John to describe it.

THE CREATION MYTHS AND THE "FALL"

The cornerstone of the sin/sacrifice/atonement doctrine is a myth. More specifically, two blended myths. Myths about the creation of our world recounted in Genesis. There can be no doubt, of course, that the stories are myths and not history. There could hardly be any eyewitnesses to creation. Moreover, well before the unknown authors penned the Genesis myths, other societies had produced similar creation stories.

But myths have power. Properly understood as myths, they may also have great value. Karen Armstrong writes that in the premodern world, myth was regarded as a form of psychology that charted the inner world. There are probably no greater testaments to the power of myth than the Jewish creation myths and the Passover myth.

Spong asserts that, through no fault of their own, Augustine and his successors did not properly understand the creation stories. At the time, they simply did not have the tools of biblical research and scholarship that later became available. They did not recognize that the two creation accounts in Genesis were written about four hundred years apart. Instead, they had come to see the Bible as a single, divinely inspired, literal document that was incapable of being inaccurate. So they merged the two creation stories, ignoring their contradictions and different implications.

In the story that appears first, on the sixth day God first creates animals and other living creatures. Later in the day, God creates men and women, at the same time and in God's image. God then pronounces everything created to be "good" and rests on the seventh day. One cannot but wonder how different Judaism and Christianity might have developed if this had been their only recorded creation story. All was well. Males and females were equal and modeled after God.

But Augustine, and others, have blended this story with an earlier, more primitive one that follows in Genesis. That story would come to be known as "the fall." The first account remains important because this second one could not make sense unless there was something from which to fall. The equality of humans and their harmony with God from the first story provided that.

In this second story, man is created first, then animals, and finally woman. Tragic as its legacy became, there is no denying an element of humor in the narrative. Once man is created, this anthropomorphic God, who had just brought our whole world into existence, saw that man was lonely and needed a companion. But the God of all creation somehow could not figure out who or what that "helpmate" should be. To the man who would be named Adam, God first makes suggestions from the ranks of animals. Karen Armstrong speculates about these exchanges: "How about a bison? An elephant? A kangaroo?" Not surprisingly, God and Adam cannot agree on a nominee.

Eventually, God puts Adam to sleep and creates the woman, to be called Eve from Adam's rib. (Many readers will recall this biblical story well. Others may recall the film with Katherine Hepburn and Spencer Tracy.)

This story concludes with Adam and Eve for a time enjoying a perfect life together in a perfect place, the garden of Eden. But then a snake appears and Eve gives in to temptation. She breaks God's command not to eat fruit of the tree of knowledge of good and evil. She persuades Adam to eat also. Thus the doctrine of "original sin" is born, along with part of the justification for the centuries of institutional misogyny to come. Eve in the story comes to be seen as the guilty one whose feminine wiles led Adam into sin, not to mention now being cast as a "helpmate" for the man rather than an equal.

God kicks the couple out of Eden. Now all descendants of the couple are likewise to be regarded as sinners in need of rescue. But what kind of rescue? Rescue from eternal responsibility for the bad acts of disobedience that the couple committed? Or rescue by provision of a doorway leading beyond their confusion to a new concept of life and living?

On these questions, common elements of power over death, sacrifice, blood, redemption and lambs came to relate the Genesis myths and Jewish rituals to the Christian crucifixion story, albeit in very different ways.

THE PASSOVER MYTH AND THE POWER OF LAMBS

On the subject of powerful beings, it is highly doubtful that one of the first that comes to mind is a lamb. It is even more unlikely that we think the power of lambs includes power over death. Would that view change if we thought about warding off death by killing lambs as a sacrifice to God? That is precisely the ritual that grew out of the history/exaggeration/myth of the liberation of the Jewish people from bondage in Egypt.

In the Exodus story, God had been visiting plagues upon Egypt in an unsuccessful attempt to persuade the Pharaoh to free the Israelites. Finally, God, in consultation with Moses, decides to kill the firstborn male in every Egyptian household, from Pharaoh right down to the flocks in the field. (Thankfully, this part of the story is not history.) To make sure only Egyptians would die, Moses tells the Jews to gather in family and neighborhood groups. Each group is to slaughter a lamb from its flock and place its blood on the doorpost. When God's angel of death comes to a home with a bloody doorpost, it will "pass over." In this way, the blood of the paschal lamb had the power to drive away the presence of death. A celebratory dinner followed where the remains of the lamb were roasted and families gathered to eat the flesh of the "lamb of God." This became the Passover observance that continues to this day.

The ease of transferring this tradition to Christian rituals like the Eucharist is obvious. Jesus and the lamb were sacrificed. The blood of each had the power to banish death. The Synoptic Gospel writers moved their Jesus story to Jerusalem at the time of Passover, making it easy to see what the Last Supper was about.

But was the death of Jesus a ritual sacrifice to bring permanent atonement for our sins? Does believing that punch our ticket to a blissful afterlife?

Or did the triumph over death that the crucifixion signifies free us to enter a new realm of consciousness—a new dimension of what it means to be human?

THE YOM KIPPUR RITUAL: THE POWER OF ANOTHER LAMB—AND A GOAT

The Passover lamb can be seen as a symbol of overcoming death through the power of blood sacrifice. Another lamb, along with perhaps a goat, symbolized something else. That lamb was part of a Jewish ritual called Yom Kippur, observed on a day called the "Day of Atonement." It still is.

Here the people addressed their yearning for wholeness, for oneness with God. Their sinful acts were only part of the separation they mourned. They acknowledged both alienation and evil. An important part of the ritual centered around hope that overcoming their alienation even symbolically, even for one day, would enhance their life experience going forward. It was not about what would happen to them when they died.

Yom Kippur proceeded as prescribed in the book of Leviticus. After a period of preparation that included fasting and confession, the people gathered at the temple, and two animals were brought in. The usual pair was a male lamb and a male goat. And not just any lamb and goat. The animals had to be physically perfect, without scratch or blemish. Further, in recognition that animals cannot choose to do evil, the two came to be seen as morally perfect as well—without sin.

The lamb was ceremonially slaughtered and its blood placed on the mercy seat in the innermost part of the temple, where God was thought to dwell. Sometimes the high priest came out and sprinkled the blood of the lamb on the people. Like the congregants centuries later in the Baptist church where I was raised, the people could sing that they had been "washed in the blood of the Lamb." They could feel at that moment that they were cleansed of sin by the power of blood. They were at one with God.

Next, the goat was brought in. The high priest took it by the horns and chanted prayers of penitence on behalf of the people, symbolically transferring their sins to the heretofore physically and morally perfect animal. The goat, now bearing the burden of their sins, came to be known as the scapegoat. Now that the animal was evil and no longer perfect, the ritual called for people to cry out that it also be killed.

But the goat was not killed. Instead, the goat was led away into the wilderness. Again, in words we hear today in Christian rituals, the goat had "taken away the sins of the world."

It appears likely that Passover and Yom Kippur had considerable influence on the way Paul and the Synoptic writers told the Jesus story. In addition to the comparisons noted, Spong calls attention to two more examples.

First, in all the Gospels, when Jesus is presented to the crowd, as was the scapegoat, the people also called for him to be killed. "Crucify him! Crucify him!"

However, all four Gospels also have a character called Barabbas whose name translates to "son of God." Thus, two sons of God. Jesus is the perfect lamb who is killed. It is Barabbas who is the goat bearing away the sins of the people.

Spong concludes that Paul's narrative was probably shaped most by Yom Kippur, though all of the Gospel writers wrote through a lens of Jewish writings and customs. Their readers would have understood the text that way. The degree to which the founders of standard Christianity understood the story that way is highly suspect.

The writers of John may well have drawn primarily on another Judaic source to tell the story of Jesus' death. Why they did so is understandable when we recognize how the situation for Christians had changed in the fifty years or so between the writings of Paul and John.

SECOND ISAIAH: A DIFFERENT KIND OF LAMB

No Old Testament text has been more useful to Christianity's effort to portray a seamless transition from Judaism than the book of Isaiah. Some of the eighth century BCE prophet's writings have been widely seen as predicting the coming of Jesus centuries later. During the Christmas season, millions of Christians thrill to the "Hallelujah Chorus" of Handel's *Messiah*, taken directly from Isaiah:

> For unto us a child is born, unto us a son is given:
> And the government shall be upon his shoulder:
> And his name shall be called Wonderful, Counsellor;
> The mighty God, The everlasting Father, The Prince of Peace
> (Isa 9:6 KJV)

Isaiah was not referring to Jesus but rather to the birth of Hezekiah, who would become not the worst king of Israel—but not the Messiah. The eloquence of the prophet's words, however, remains a powerful inspiration for Christians.

But, a different writer penned chapters 40–55 of Isaiah. Unknown, the writer has come to be referred to as Second Isaiah. This portrait of a giver of hope differs remarkably from the one upon which Handel drew to compose his masterpiece.

The person to whom Second Isaiah refers is seen as a "suffering servant." This image is consistent with New Christianity. And the situation from which this Messiah arose is similar to that faced centuries later by the writers of John and members of their Christian community.

The different vision of Second Isaiah is most apparent in chapter 53. There, the influence of Yom Kippur may again be seen. The portrait, however, is of a lamb that is not only slaughtered but also assumes the role of the scapegoat ("Yahweh burdened him with the sins of all of us" [Isa 53:6]).

There is an extensive description of the lamb and the circumstances of his death. This is not the mighty counsellor or king of kings. Rather, the lamb suffers injustice and death in silence, producing a new and arguably different kind of Messiah prophesy: "Harshly dealt with, he never opened his mouth. Like a lamb that is led to the slaughterhouse" (Isa 53:7).

This Messiah is part of an adjustment that Jews returning from the humiliating exile in Babylon had to make. Their aspirations had always gone beyond the personal to encompass a mighty role for Judah and Israel. Through the power wielded as God's chosen people they would be a blessing to the world. But the returning exiles would find that dream shattered. Jerusalem and the temple were rubble. The future of the Jews was to be weakness. As a nation, they would never again be a significant power.

Second Isaiah responded to this situation with a new image of how the Jews could still be a blessing to the world. Like the lamb in chapter 53, they would turn weakness into an expression of a new purpose. Spong sees it as this: *They would drain the world of its anger by absorbing it and then returning it as love.*

In the remainder of Isaiah, the prophet inspires hope, describing how this new role for the people will produce better times, a New Jerusalem.

The life of Jesus mirrored this new vision of the Messiah. He showed the world the meaning of love by silently taking on the anger, pain, and death inflicted on him.

Unfortunately, history has shown that the idea of a suffering servant role for Israel and its messiah has not taken hold. It is certainly not the role chosen by the modern nation of Israel. In Jesus' time images of power and violence dominated. The Pax Romana of the Roman Empire was based on achieving order and peace by conquering and brutally subjugating peoples. "Peace through strength" today echoes that image.

So it was also in the time of John's early Christian community. Oppression by Rome and its surrogate rulers continued and may have made it easier to grasp a mystical understanding of the Messiah of Second Isaiah.

When John's Gospel appeared in the nineties CE, Rome still ruled violently, and a violent Jewish response had failed. A Jewish Zealot rebellion in 66 had been brutally suppressed, and the temple had again been destroyed in 70.

There was perhaps an even greater concern for those who had been awaiting the dramatic coda to the atonement narrative. Jesus had not returned as promised to establish a holy kingdom that would do away with evil. It had been sixty-five to seventy years since the crucifixion and the bad times had not ended. Think of those today who might have believed a 1959 street preacher who claimed that the world would end in glory in 2024.

Spong concludes that in this context, John changed the sin and salvation message and radically transformed the story of Jesus' death. He did not die to pay the price for sin. He did not promise to come again out of the heavens and establish the kingdom of God. He would not be a king in the sense that people understood the term. He would have no army. The answer to their longing would not be peace through strength. Instead, he died to open life to a new meaning and a new definition. The kingdom of God was already here. His death was his glory, the moment God was fully revealed in him.

Again, perhaps that is why the little snippet in the feeding of the multitude story deserves more attention than it gets. Jesus fled a crowd that wanted to start a movement. Thousands wanted to make him a conquering king in the literal terms they understood. By the time John was written, it should have been plain that the crowd did not understand. This was not what the Jesus story was about. It was the death of God's chosen human, not the death of his enemies that was important.

In the final account of the first discourse, Jesus undertakes to explain this to the disciples, giving three of them the role of questioners.

The first is Thomas. Jesus has offered comforting words, telling the disciples not to be troubled, telling them that he is going to prepare a place for them and that they now know the way to the place he is going.

Thomas, perhaps even yet trapped in literalism, protests that they do not know where Jesus is going, so how could they know the way?

Jesus responds with the words that Marcus Borg describes as the centuries-old "proof text" for Christian exclusivism: "I am the Way, the Truth, and the Life. No one can come to the Father except through me" (John 14:6). As noted, this verse is even today used as proof that salvation is possible only through Jesus and thus only through Christianity.

But as Borg and Spong recognize, throughout the discourses Jesus is trying to teach the disciples that a way is a path on a journey and not a set of beliefs. He is telling them that the journey is not outward but inward. God is not up there. God is in here. As he will show, to discover how to give yourself is the pathway to the Father.

Philip is next, and he asks about the destination—the Father. He says that if Jesus will let them see the Father, then they will all be satisfied.

Jesus is understandably a bit disappointed that at this late date the disciples cannot see his oneness with God and with them. Neither can they see their own oneness with God and what it can mean in their lives.

Jesus explains again that he is in the Father and the Father is in him. What he says to them comes not from him but from the Father. God is doing the work. He tells them that when they understand this, they will go on to do even greater things than he has done.

He comforts them further with an assurance that his death will not mean that they are left alone. He will return to them as a spirit of love and truth, and they will then understand that "I am in my Father, and you in me and I in you" (John 14:20). They will understand the mystery and achieve this dimension of life if they obey his commandments: to love, not for gain but for love's sake.

The final question is from Judas (who the Gospel makes clear is not Judas Iscariot). He wants to know if this new destiny Jesus has described is to be available to the world or just to them. Jesus' answer is "anyone." Anyone who keeps the commandments of love. But he tells them to remember that this experience is internal, not external. It comes with the growing ability to love beyond what you see as your limits. But when you succeed, God and I will come and make our homes in you.

These remarkable exchanges show Jesus as at once teaching the disciples and us, as well as comforting them. He concludes by reminding Judas of the spirit that God will send to continue his teaching and remind them of his words. He urges them again not to let their hearts be troubled or afraid. If they can accept it, he leaves to them a peace that the world cannot understand.

Finally, he prepares them for his death by telling them that the worldly powers are coming soon to kill him, but this is necessary so that the world may know that he loves the Father and is doing exactly what the Father has asked.

However much or little the disciples grasped this message from the one into whom they had poured their hopes, this must have been a heart-wrenching moment.

Their leader had told them that he was going away but not to a physical place on earth or "up there." He had promised to return to them, but he didn't say when. He promised to send them a spirit that would teach them. How would that work?

Perhaps most unsettling of all, he had told them that his way of learning to love beyond limits was an internal path to seeing his oneness with God and with them. Any who followed it would do great works of love and would find peace.

John's Gospel, especially the preamble, John 3:16–17, and John 14:6, has been seen as a bulwark of standard atonement theology. New Christianity sees it through a very different lens, telling a very different story.

As these teachings and his life near their end, it is important for Jesus to reinforce his empowering message of oneness, his warnings, and his gift of hope. It is also important that he do it in a way that those familiar with Judaism can grasp. And so, the farewell discourses move to conclusion.

CHAPTER 19

The Analogy of the Vine

God Is Indwelling, Not External

IN DESCRIBING THIS FINAL teaching session with the disciples, John's writers have Jesus use a familiar Jewish image to impress upon them his message of universal spiritual oneness. We see him teaching about the driving force underlying oneness and how it can work in their lives. We see him warning that those who understand and live this teaching will be persecuted and why. Yet his final words are words of comfort. He promises that when he is gone, he will send his spirit to guide them on this new path.

To make clear the message of spiritual oneness, Jesus analogizes to an image that would be familiar to those trained in Judaism. The prophets had often referred to the people of Israel as "God's vineyard." Even though the audience was familiar with the analogy, the task of getting the point across was formidable. It would require contradicting what Jews had been taught to view as the relationship between God and humans.

They had been taught that there were two realms. God was an external being in an external location. This externality continued when God chose to connect with humans. God intervened in human history, speaking directly to influential actors from Adam and Eve onward—Moses, Noah, Abraham, etc. God could come down to earth, but humans could not lift themselves to God. Jesus' version of how "God's vineyard" was constructed and operated in the world reflected a very different vision of the relationship.

PART III | THE FAREWELL DISCOURSES

Jesus tells his followers to think of God as the vinedresser, tending the vine so that life can flow through it. Jesus is the vine, the human life in whom God is present. The symbol of a New Jerusalem, one that embodies a nonviolent blessing for the world. They are the branches of the vine.

The comparison illustrates oneness. If the branches stay attached, all three elements will be one. But the analogy also demonstrates how a vineyard works. Jesus is the human life in whom the life of God is present. God flows through him. He tells them that, as the branches, if they abide in him and his words, they too will become the word of God incarnate.

Further, in this spiritual unity there may be different levels of awareness, but there is not a hierarchy of subservience. Jesus tells them he will no longer call them servants but friends.

In their lives this new oneness will have all parts of the vine acting together in furtherance of a new mission, a new creation. Jesus assures them that if they continue in unity and if they abide in him, his words will abide in them.

He tells them that the absolute key to this relationship is love. Their joy will be complete if they can learn to love one another as he has loved them. Note that the commandment is to love one another *as* he has loved them, not *because* he first loved them, as the children's song goes. The challenge is to love in a way and to a degree that is beyond the limits they have known to that point.

This is, of course, not the first time the disciples have been present to hear Jesus speak of love. They were there when Jesus explained through the parable of the good Samaritan that there were no ethnic, national, or racial limits to the commandment to love. That everyone was the neighbor we are commanded to love (Luke 10:25–37).

Immediately after repeating the commandment to love one another as much as he has loved them, Jesus gives them an example. It is an example that is a distinctive element of New Christianity, distinguishing it from the standard narrative. He tells them that one can have no greater love than to lay down one's life for others.

The farewell discourses end on a very positive note. The disciples are said as one to proclaim that they now understand that Jesus came from God. There is no need to use metaphors. They understand his plain words.

Jesus expresses some benign skepticism about this but concludes by saying, "I have told you all this so that you may find peace in me. In the world you will have trouble, but be brave: I have conquered the world."

Both the external "atonement" understanding of the Jesus story and John's internal vision can, with some inconsistencies, be overlaid with Judaism. But one problem with the former, a problem Spong does not mention, is the importance of the afterlife to atonement theology. Jesus died for our sins so that we could go up to heaven when we die and not down to hell. But Judaism doesn't seem to concern itself very much with an afterlife. Sheol was a dank realm, not very pleasant but no eternal fire and brimstone. The Old Testament God punished people for their sins, but the retribution took place for the most part during their time on earth.

The emerging atonement story of course had an effect on the early Johannine Christians. But a larger problem with it arose. It was now more than 90 years since the death of Jesus. Those who took literally his promise to return "soon" could not help but be apprehensive. Nine decades had passed. Christians had died. Jesus had not come back. Which of the two atonement story fates awaited them?

More than forty years earlier this had already become such a concern that Paul was moved to construct an explanation. He still anticipated that Jesus would return in his lifetime. However, he wanted to comfort one of his anxious congregations. He told them that those living when Jesus returned would not have any advantage over believers who had died in the interim. With great fanfare, Jesus would return and take both groups up in the clouds to be with him forever. In fact, those who had died in Christ would go up first, ahead of the living believers.

But time went on. Jesus did not return. Paul's assurance was little help. Later, wittingly or not, Luke gave a boost to standard theological literalism and externalism by theorizing that the second coming was really the birth of the church. That had to happen before the coming of Jesus. In Acts, he went on to write about the growth and development of the early church. Over the next few centuries, the institutional founding fathers picked it up from there.

The external Jesus has yet to return. But John's story does not depend on that ever happening. There is a very different story to be found in the final discourses as the writers of the John's Gospel saw them. Jesus is not coming back in the manner that some early Christians thought. He has already shown the way to oneness, to abundant life.

His teaching ministry complete, Jesus now turns to his own relationship with God as he prepares for the time when he will be "lifted up," when he will demonstrate the highest degree of love.

CHAPTER 20

The Prayer of Jesus

Gethsemane Transformed

BETWEEN THE FINAL DISCOURSES and the passion story, John places a prayer. The Synoptics have Jesus in the garden of Gethsemane, praying that God reconsider his impending fate but reaffirming his commitment to God's divine will.

That episode does not appear in John. Rather, Jesus prays for himself, his disciples, and for all those in the coming centuries who will be transformed by what will happen here. The mystical themes of the prayer are those that have been portrayed throughout the Fourth Gospel: Radical Inclusion. Universal Oneness. Love.

There is little need for extensive commentary on the powerful words of this prayer. The words John has Jesus say speak eloquently.

Jesus acknowledges that the hour of his glorification is near and willingly accepts it so that God may be glorified by it, as he will be. He asks that God grant eternal life to all who have been entrusted to him and speaks of eternal life as a present transformation, not a future trip to somewhere after death: "And eternal life is this: to know you, the only true God, and Jesus Christ whom you have sent" (John 17:3–4).

He gives thanks that his followers have understood the teaching that God has given to him. He acknowledges that the world will hate them because they are perceived as different and asks God to protect them. Through the ages, perceived differences have engendered fear, hatred, and violence. He asks that his followers be consecrated in the truth of the word he has brought.

The prayer concludes by touching all three themes. Jesus prays that all who hear and believe the way of love that he is showing will over the centuries be united in awareness that they are one with the divine. Again, he does not claim to be the only Way-Shower but pleads on behalf of those who will come to follow his path:

"Father, may they be one in us, as you are in me and I am in you . . . that they may be one as we are one. With me in them and you in me" . . . (John 17:21–23).

Finally, Jesus speaks of the powerful interconnectedness of love that is the foundation of oneness and radical inclusion. He asks that all who follow his way, whenever they find it,

> may be one as we are one. With me in them and you in me, may they be so completely one that the world will realize that it was you who sent me and that I have loved them as much as you loved me . . . so that the love with which you loved me may be in them, and so that I may be in them. (John 17:22–24, 26)

Spong concludes this chapter by reaffirming its significance to New Christianity. Rather than accept the guilt-ridden mantra of sin and sacrifice, we should see that

> *we do not need to be rescued, but to experience the power of an all-embracing love . . . Our call is to move from a status of self-consciousness to a realization that we share in a universal consciousness . . . That is the meaning to which the signs in John's gospel point.*

As John's Gospel story moves to its conclusion, it will explore one of the most stunning aspects of New Christianity. Spong offers a preview:

> *John's rendition of Jesus' message is that the essence of life is discovered when one is free to give life away, that love is known in the act of loving.*

PART IV

The Passion Narrative

*From Darkness to Light,
from Death to Life*

CHAPTER 21

A Brief Introduction to the Climax of This Gospel

THIS IS ANOTHER SHORT "reminder" chapter. It is needed because of the particular importance of understanding the context of John's writing about the final act of the drama.

We are reminded to read the Gospel at two non-literal levels. Read it as part of the Jesus story in the time of Jesus. Perhaps even more importantly, read it also as how the beleaguered Johannine Christians may have seen the story and how it affected their plight.

Spong obviously considers grasping this second level as essential to understanding the Gospel story as a whole. Consequently, he reviews in some detail the history and experience of the writers of the Fourth Gospel.

The Christian movement was born in the synagogue. Jewish Christians worked to expand Judaism to include acceptance of Jesus as at least a major prophet. They worked to relate Jesus to early heroes like Abraham, Moses, and Elijah.

Naturally, such a major proposal caused tension in the synagogue. But the parties seemed to be working it out until violence disrupted the process. The Jewish rebellion against Rome in 66 CE resulted in Roman destruction of the Jerusalem temple in 70 and final defeat of the Jews at Masada in

PART IV | THE PASSION NARRATIVE

73. The rebellion was brutally crushed, and Judaism was left in desperate straits.

In this new reality, there was no longer room to tolerate internal tensions. Around 88 CE the Christians were expelled from the synagogue. Now they found themselves outside Judaism! It is understandable that these Christians were angry at those who had tossed them out. This explains in part the derogatory references in the Gospel to "the Jews," which later generations of misguided Christians turned into virulent antisemitism.

Whatever the state of their collective animosity, the members of this Christian community now faced the challenge of defining themselves as quite separate from Judaism.

This challenge led to internal tensions and divisions. How far could the community go with Jesus as more than a prophet or Judaic hero? How far could they go in speaking about Jesus as a "God experience" without losing members who were still loyal to Judaism? Would such members ever get to a place where they could accept Jesus' claim of oneness with God, of his adoption of the sacred name "I AM"?

The internal divisions deepened and some members left and returned to traditional Judaism. Some of those who remained reviled them as traitors, but some in the core community were faithful to a developing new vision.

This is the context of the passion story in John. The storytellers are part of a community that is standing alone in the face of the formidable institutions of Judaism and the Roman Empire, as well as internal crises. The characters in their story represent actors in this time of conflict and tension. Pilate, for example, is the story's representative of their relationship with Rome. The conversation between Jesus and Pilate is about issues facing the Christian community at the time of the Gospel-writing.

So Spong reminds us that rather than being a literal account, the story is *the painting of an interpretive portrait by a devoted artist*. It is in this passion narrative that the writers of John lay out the new Gospel that a part of the community was beginning to develop in the midst of turmoil. It represents an effort to *bind together the former Jewish expectations with a new sense of God as mystical oneness.*

CHAPTER 22

Judas

The Figure of Darkness

IN OUR CONSIDERATION OF Judas and the other characters in the passion story we see the value of Spong's reminders in the previous chapter. The writers of John were part of a Christian community that was rife with internal division even as it stood alone in dangerous times.

Although he posits that deciding whether Judas was a real figure or a literary device is not essential to understanding his role, Spong devotes considerable space to arguments for the latter reading. He cites various sources but again relies greatly on the significance of what Paul left out. Paul recounted a visit with Peter three years after his conversion. The visit included a conversation with Peter in which a disciple, James, the brother of Jesus, participated. There is nothing reported about Judas. Spong concludes that if Judas Iscariot had been part of the memory of the early Christians, Paul would surely have mentioned him.

Paul does, of course, write to the churches about the surrender of Jesus. But he speaks of Jesus being "handed over," not "betrayed." In Paul's instructions about proper observance of the Lord's Supper he does use the word "betrayed" but never "betrayer" or Judas by name or any of the disciples. Indeed, in the same letter to the church at Corinth he tells of Jesus appearing to Peter and 12 twelve disciples three days after the crucifixion.

Whether historical or literary, Judas has two important roles in the passion story. He stands for the Jews who were persecuting both Jesus and the later Johannine Christians. His acts are part of that relationship in both time frames, as well as part of the accommodation of official Jewry with the Roman powers.

More importantly, Judas is a symbol of the interplay of light and darkness that has been so important to the way John tells the Jesus story. He binds together many of the sign stories about Jesus the Way-Shower's offer of transformative, abundant life. In this context Judas has an important place on the continuum of inclusion and rejection experiences that we have seen in the earlier stories. It is worthwhile to review the earlier stories of those who have been offered the way into the light.

Consider again, for example, the conversation with Nicodemus. He was a learned man, with most of life's advantages. But something impelled him to seek out Jesus. Their conversation eventually did get beyond literalism. Sadly, however, he was always close to the presence of light but could not enter it. Ultimately, perhaps he could not yet grasp that a kingdom was more of an experience than a place. That the experience could be a radical new awareness of our unity and a mystical sense of identity with God.

Nicodemus was offered immediate inclusion in such a kingdom, but he could not bring himself to leave his comfortable life as it was. A Pharisee, ensconced in a respected religion, he may have concluded that such radical change was simply not worth it.

However, as close to synagogue authorities as he was, Nicodemus took no further action against Jesus. And he later appears in the story, still conflicted. Recall that this was not the case with the man crippled for thirty-eight years.

That story is followed by two more stories showing Jesus' offer of radical inclusion in the mystical kingdom being accepted. First by a person who is not only a Samaritan but also a woman. Then by the gentile official's son, representing every non-Jew on the planet.

Alas, then comes the story of the man crippled for thirty-eight years who cannot seem to get to the folkloric healing pool in time. This story culminates with a revealing exchange between Jesus and Jewish officials. But the character of the crippled man also provides a step in the inclusion/rejection continuum.

To this point, Jesus has offered inclusion to all sorts and conditions of people. Socially, the man at the pool occupied the lowest status of them all. We do not know much about him other than his revealing trait of always blaming something else for his misfortune. As he repeatedly returned to the pool one wonders whether, subconsciously, he was more comfortable with that routine. Did he ever really give thought to what being healed would be like?

That may well be why Jesus asked if he wished to be healed. It may be why he responded with his standard excuse. That may be why Jesus ignored the excuse and healed him on the spot. Now there was no excuse not to enter the frightening new world of inclusion in the kingdom that Jesus offered. Opening himself to wholeness, he trembles because he can no longer hide his fears inside the excuses of his past.

Unlike Nicodemus and all the other characters to this point, the man does not ask anything further of or about the source of this life-changing event. He simply picks up his pallet and beats a quick retreat. He thus avoids hearing more from Jesus about the new dimension of life being offered to him.

So, when the synagogue leaders confront the man about breaking the Sabbath, it is no surprise that his response is another excuse, on the order of "I'm not responsible. I just did what the man told me to do." He was probably relieved to be able to testify truthfully that he did not know the identity of the man who had told him to take up his pallet and walk. He hurried off to the temple, perhaps to give thanks as much for getting out of a tough scrape as for his new mobility.

But Jesus sought him out there, warned him not to regress to his old ways and probably tried to speak further with him. Yet the man left again. This time, unlike Nicodemus, he did not just retreat to his old life to build a new security system and think of new excuses. Instead, he went back to the authorities and named Jesus as the one who had cured him.

In the conversation that followed with the Jewish officials, the more serious issue of Jesus' relationship with God came up, and it was from that point that they began to plot his death.

Nicodemus heard and walked away. But that is all he did. The crippled man at the pool knew nothing of the message and rejected all efforts to even hear about how to be included in a new dimension of life. He also walked away. But before he did, he perhaps unknowingly put the life of Jesus in danger.

Finally, we come to Judas, who had been immersed in the light and enjoyed the ultimate level of inclusion. He was one of the twelve. Yet he went further into the darkness than the man at the pool.

PART IV | THE PASSION NARRATIVE

The best remembered account of Judas, of course, is at the Last Supper. But he had appeared six days earlier when Jesus visited the home of Mary and Martha. There we find that he was already turning from light toward darkness. He had a trusted position as keeper of the common funds of the twelve but was embezzling.

In John's Gospel, the Last Supper happened at night. The transition of Judas was completed. Jesus told him to act quickly. Judas then departed immediately into the night. Only in John did he return with Roman soldiers as well as officers from the chief priests and Pharisees. They carried lanterns and torches, ineffective as tools to ward off the enveloping darkness.

The symbolism of those who came could not be plainer, both for Jesus and the Johannine Christians. Judas' name is the name of the Jewish nation, Judah. The word "Jew" means citizen of Judea. In this story, Jesus as well as the early Christians were quite isolated.

And yet, it is here that the story begins to turn not to gloom but to glory. Jesus asked whom they sought. When they responded "Jesus of Nazareth," he said "I AM," invoking again the name for God revealed in Exodus. Hearing this, his pursuers drew back and fell to the ground.

This exchange is so significant that it is repeated in the story. But together, the Jewish and Roman contingent eventually make the arrest and bring Jesus before Annas, the high priest.

There is no further mention of Judas. From a special place of inclusion, he had been offered a doorway into a new dimension of life and love. Like Nicodemus and the man at the pool, he could not risk leaving the comfort and security of the way things were. When the light came too close to Judas, however, instead of retreating from it he tried to extinguish it. So it may be with many today.

The chapter closes with reflections on light and darkness. One reminder is that light does not destroy darkness. Rather, it shines within it, and the darkness cannot extinguish it. The rest of the story may well be consistent with that view.

CHAPTER 23

Peter

The Struggle Within the Soul

THERE WAS ANOTHER WHO, like Judas, had lived and experienced the doorway out of self-consciousness into a new dimension of love, of oneness with God and with others. Peter did not sadly walk away as did Nicodemus. He did not carelessly put Jesus in danger like the man at the pool. He did not actively seek to aid those pursuing Jesus as did Judas. But neither did he quickly grasp the import of the door Jesus was opening as did the Samaritan woman at the well.

Rather, the literary figure of Peter is a representative of all of us. His courage and his understanding were hindered by the same human factors that hinder ours. Like Peter, we all face the obstacles of fear and insecurity when we are invited to make life-altering choices. Our worldview is composed of elements that provide security and a bulwark against fear. We cherish them. Like Peter, we know that there is something within us that wants to become. We know there is more. But also like Peter, we want to survive. We are the center of us. As Pogo said in the famous cartoon that appeared after the murder of John F. Kennedy: "We have met the enemy, and he is us."

To greater or lesser degrees, we brag to hide our fear. We lie to cover our inadequacies. We push others down to elevate ourselves. In fact, we construct elaborate justifications for supporting violence against others. We love no one more than ourselves. We are spirits, but our human experience presents us all with the diverse frailties of humankind.

These are not sins, the expiation of which require someone to come down from the sky, then die and rise again in a manner we will later ritualize. We see how inadequately that has worked out over the centuries to combat actions born of our fear and insecurity. Instead, the way is open to learn to have life and have it more abundantly by embracing a new dimension of what it means to be human.

Peter eventually understood, but his understanding was not immediate, and it was not easy. He shared with us the fruits of fear and insecurity that I have described. But Peter's story should be particularly encouraging for those who at one point have sought to address them by being part of Christianity, or any faith community, and found the experience singularly unhelpful.

If Peter, who had been privileged to walk in the light the whole way, could not easily grasp a new way, how much more understandable the disaffection of those today who have sampled standard Christianity and found it wanting. But Peter kept on. In his confusion, in his worst hours, something within Peter told him that he could become rather than simply exist.

Peter's story should also be good news for those who have never seen a need to turn to a faith community to deal with fear and insecurity. After all, to dismantle the walls of security they have managed to build would be an intimidating, even frightening move. Why risk it if "religion" has nothing to offer? If it is in essence just superstition, easily debunked by our powers of reason?

It must have also been a scary thing for Peter, then called Simon. He was a prosperous Galilean fisherman, married with a family, doing quite well. His Greek name suggests he lived and did business in highly Hellenized Bethsaida. Indeed, John tells us that Simon and his brother Andrew came from that town. All in all, it appears he had a pretty good security system in place.

Yet he dropped all this and became the follower of an itinerant stranger. His brother Andrew, moved by the witness of John the Baptist, introduced him to Jesus, who gave him the name Peter. John provides a more detailed account than the other Gospels of this beginning but leaves us with many questions. Andrew is said to have brought the word that Jesus was the Messiah. But none of the Gospels tell us anything about Peter's prior experience, if any, with organized religion. Assuming he believed his brother, how could that be enough to explain what came next? Was it the power of accepting that Jesus was the one of whom the prophets had spoken? Was there something apart from his conversation with Jesus that prompted him to put aside his security system and make the life-altering decision to be one of what would come to be called "the Twelve"?

Whatever the reason, this has to be seen as a major act of courage. It may also hold another lesson for us. Opting for a radical new life path does not solve everything instantly. Peter would eventually learn transformative love and become something of a way-shower himself. But it did not happen when he answered Jesus' call. Indeed, we will see that the understanding and import of Jesus as the way, the truth, and the life did not fully mature in Peter, even though he was a first hand witness to Jesus' life and teaching. This venture was always scary. The security of the old life was always there in the background. Fear was always present.

The story of Peter's ultimate understanding does not come to a conclusion in this chapter. Rather, as the chapter title suggests, it is about the struggle within his soul.

It is a struggle many experience today. They know that the path to awareness is not a straight line. Peter exemplified that.

The ignorance of all the disciples about what might lay before them mirrors that of many of us who recognize a potentially big change but see it only in the context of what we already think we know. Peter and the disciples became followers of one who would open the door to a new life, but understanding of it was slowed by their self-consciousness of the only life they knew.

Peter and the others may have been motivated initially by a belief that Jesus was the Messiah. The person that their Jewish education had taught them would come to establish the kingdom of God. The first indication that this "kingdom" would be quite different from the one about which they had been taught may have come from the Samaritan woman at the well. Jesus' encounter with her happened at a place of significance in Jewish society, but it certainly did not jibe with the traditional Messiah story. Radical inclusion was not part of that story. As we have seen, Peter and the disciples were more than a little surprised at Jesus speaking not only with a woman but a Samaritan. It is possible that this potentially scary departure from the norms of life began to alert Peter that there was something new on the horizon.

PART IV | THE PASSION NARRATIVE

But Peter's journey to understanding was slow, and his struggle to become was difficult. It reached its low point at the arrest of Jesus and its immediate aftermath.

Earlier, Peter had loudly objected to the idea of Jesus washing his feet. He did not understand this symbolic upset of the social order, even when Jesus explained: "If I do not wash your feet, you can have nothing in common with me."

Peter's slow journey to understanding continues when the Jewish and Roman representatives arrest Jesus. Peter shows that he does not yet understand that nonviolence is part of the new kingdom. He draws his sword and cuts off the ear of one of the high priest's men.

But the power of the new path he had been shown grew within Peter. When Jesus was taken away to Annas, father-in-law of the high priest, Peter did not seize this chance to get away and seek to rebuild the security of his old life. Along with one other disciple, about whom we will later hear much, Peter followed Jesus to the palace of the high priest.

It was there, however, that fear and the desire for survival asserted themselves again most forcefully. It was there that Peter reached the nadir of his dedication to the new way that he had so courageously undertaken. The story of how that unfolded tells us much.

Peter went to the palace but elected to stay outside the door. Fear had put him symbolically outside the door that Jesus had opened for him. The other disciple later brought Peter inside. At this point we see that although Peter was consumed by fear, there was no real threat. A United States president once captured Peter's position by saying, "The only thing we have to fear is fear itself." We can see the truth of this by noting those to whom Peter spoke the words of denial that Jesus had foretold.

The first was only a maid on duty when Peter came inside. She asked, "Aren't you another of that man's disciples?" Peter said he was not and went to join others who were warming themselves at a charcoal fire. Fear sometimes prompts us to try losing ourselves in the crowd. But the one who challenged him here was but a lowly maidservant, not an agent of either Rome or Judaism. There was no reason to give such a fear-laden response.

Likewise, Peter's second denial of Jesus came while he was with others at the fire. The same question the maid had asked produced the same response. This time the question was put by a questioner simply described as "someone." If Peter perceived a threat here, it could only have come from the tendency of fear to provoke imaginary ones.

Finally, one of the servants of the high priest asked the question in a slightly different form. He was a relative of the man Peter had attacked with his sword and asked, "Didn't I see you in the garden with him?" On one hand, the question is not in itself incriminating. It is not an accusation of assault. On the other, an honest response and further questions might lead to danger. Heading off even what we foresee as possible threats is also part of our security system. Peter denied Jesus again. Then he went back to fishing.

But the power of the way he had been shown would prevail, as we will see in the final words of John's Gospel. There Peter will come to understand that we are part of who God is, and God is part of who we are; that the life of God is found in our living; that the love of God is found in our loving.

For now, we leave a fearful and confused Peter as we resume the passion story.

CHAPTER 24

Pilate

The Conflict Between Survival and Truth

This chapter is aptly named. It recounts an amazing conflict between survival and truth. Truth prevails. At the conclusion of the events following the arrest of Jesus there is nothing left of the power of religion or the state over him. The authority and security systems of both are severely shaken.

The drama unfolds when Jesus is taken before Pilate, the Roman governor of Judea, from 26–36 CE. We know little about Pilate, although what is known does not suggest any likelihood that conversations with Jesus such as those depicted in the Gospel could have happened. Here the conversations are literary devices, but the characters are real historical figures. There is much to learn. At this point New Christianity begins to diverge even more from standard doctrines.

The Gospels, including John, move increasingly toward portraying Pilate in a relatively sympathetic light as one who was reluctant to allow the execution of Jesus. Some later writers even had him becoming a Christian and willingly being beheaded for his role in the death of Jesus. By the sixth century CE, Coptic Christians considered him a saint. Keep in mind, however, that Rome was the one earthly power the Gospel writers had to face. After the suppression of the rebellion and the second destruction of the temple, the Jews were completely subject to Rome as the only temporal power. That reality may be the most important factor in the benign Gospel treatment of Pilate. The Romans were a brutal lot, and one did not want to provoke them unnecessarily. But the assignment of that reluctant role to Pilate also helped the writers of John tell their very different Jesus story.

Before his meeting with Jesus, Pilate could hardly be said to have been a friend to the ordinary Jew. He had good relations with the Jerusalem aristocracy and priesthood, but that regard did not extend to respect for the general Jewish population under his rule. Luke wrote of "the Galileans whose blood Pilate had mingled with their sacrifices." Though he had a long tenure as governor, Pilate was eventually relieved of his post and ordered back to Rome for massacring a group of Samaritans. Other early writers complained of his cruelty.

This background raises real questions about what happened when Pilate faced Jesus. The chief priests brought Jesus to Pilate because they wanted him killed and the details of their law in relation to Rome forbade them from carrying out executions.

The Jewish officials would not enter the courthouse. It was considered unclean, and entry would mean they could not participate in the coming Passover. Pilate kindly comes outside to meet them. He inquires of the charges. The officials, however, answer with a line that many today unthinkingly see as acceptable. In essence, they respond, "Never mind charges and evidence. If he wasn't a guilty criminal, we wouldn't have brought him here." In further response to Pilate's statement that they should deal with him themselves, they then explain that they want Jesus executed but cannot do it themselves.

Based on what we know of Pilate, should not one expect that he would just accept their explanation, give permission for the execution, and move on to the next case? All in a day's work.

But in John's account, Pilate is reluctant to authorize the execution. Instead, he goes back inside the Praetorium. Jesus, who transcended Jewish purity laws, follows. There ensues an amazing three-way exchange among Pilate, Jesus, and those gathered outside.

Pilate asks Jesus if he is the king of the Jews. Jesus perceives that this is something that Pilate must have heard about. Pilate implicitly acknowledges this by saying all he knows is what he has heard and reminds Jesus that it is his own people who have handed him over. Jesus then tells Pilate that yes, he is a king, but his kingdom is of a different kind. It is not a kingdom of this world. He reminds Pilate that if kings and kingdoms were to be understood in the usual way, his followers would have fought to prevent his arrest. We are reminded again of the feeding of the five thousand, where Jesus hid from those who sought to make him king.

He confirms his mission as Way-Shower, telling Pilate that he came into the world to bear witness to the truth. He came to show the way to living a life that is beyond religion and beyond the temporal powers. He had already given the essence of this teaching to Jewish officials and to his Jewish followers, telling them that if they make his word their home, they will learn the truth, and the truth would make them free (John 8:13–32). There is nothing eschatological in this exchange. Jesus may be speaking of a kingdom unlike that of the popular understanding of the term, but he is also speaking of his kingdom as a new dimension of life here and now, not someday.

Understandably, Pilate could not grasp the import of Jesus' words. But the way the episode continues suggests that he was deeply affected by this glimpse into the real identity and purpose of Jesus. It is no surprise that Pilate did not understand. Instead, he too fell back on an abstract escape route. It is one that is part of the security system for many of us, especially those of us who pride ourselves on having the intellect to recognize abstractions. Pilate asks rhetorically, "What is truth?" and takes Jesus outside again to face his accusers.

Affected by what he had heard but now comfortable again in his legal role, Pilate tells the Jews that they have no case. But perhaps not wanting to severely alienate the Jewish officialdom with whom he enjoyed good relations, he reminds them of their custom of releasing one prisoner at Passover and asks if they wish release for the "king of the Jews."

The officials reply that they would rather have the release of a brigand called Barabbas. We have looked at Barabbas before in the context of Jewish rituals. (It should be noted here also that Roman brutality and taxation in those days made a lot of honest men brigands.)

Pilate still wants to avoid imposing the death penalty. He has Jesus taken away and scourged. Jesus is also mocked by the guards and made to wear a robe and a crown of thorns, all to ridicule his claim to be king of the Jews. Hoping that this would be enough, Pilate brings Jesus outside. There he is displayed as a ridiculous, powerless "king." Pilate once again tells the chief priests that they have no case.

The drama concludes with three very important developments: assignment of responsibility for the crucifixion, the powerlessness of Rome, and the final surrender of Judaism.

The writers of John wished to make clear that responsibility for the crucifixion of Jesus rests primarily upon the Jewish hierarchy. This view has had serious repercussions over the years. As we have noted more than once, the use of the term "the Jews" in the Gospel is a reference to that hierarchy and not to ordinary Jewry, of which the writers were a part. They are not responsible for the antisemitic violence in later centuries. Further, there is much evidence that violence against Jews is usually motivated more by political considerations than religious ones.

In this story, however, it is clearly the Jewish power structure in Jerusalem that bears responsibility, and there is no getting around that. In John's account it is the chief priests not the people in the crowd who cry, "Crucify him!" In Matthew, the chief priests persuade the crowd to cry out.

After telling them again that they have no case against Jesus, Pilate gives up and says, "Go ahead and crucify him." Oddly, however, the story does not end there. Perhaps the officials are uneasy about their relationship with the Romans. What if they go ahead when even the one who gave grudging permission had told them they were going to kill an innocent man? For some reason, they feel the need to justify themselves and so continue to speak.

They assert that they have a law requiring that Jesus be put to death because he claims to be the Son of God. They may have been speaking generally about an interpretation of Torah. There was, however, no such specific law. This pronouncement in turn increases Pilate's anxiety about the whole matter sufficiently that he decides further interrogation of Jesus is warranted. This time Jesus declines to participate, prompting Pilate to remind him that he holds the power to release him or have him crucified.

Jesus responds with his own reminder, telling Pilate that he would be without such power had it not been given to him from above. The state has now played its trump card and gotten nowhere. Jesus is not moved at all by Pilate's threat to use its ultimate power.

Here there is some further indication that the meeting with Jesus has an impact on Pilate. John writes that from this moment he is anxious to set Jesus free. But at this point, the Jews play their own trump card. They shout that Pilate would be no friend of Caesar's if he releases Jesus. The last thing a provincial governor needs is a complaint to Rome about a troubled relationship with the empire's subjects. When Pilate tells them to take their king away, the chief priests respond, "We have no king but Caesar." This is a desperate and damaging concession.

PART IV | THE PASSION NARRATIVE

The representatives of Judaism here abandon the religion of Abraham, a faith tradition that included centuries of kings who pledged separation from any power save Yahweh. They cede their last claim to being a messianic people. All to secure the right to execute one man.

An exhausted Pilate hands Jesus over to them to be crucified.

The story continues on the subject of kings and kingdoms that are quite different from the kings and kingdoms understood by the Romans and Jews at that time and by much of Christianity in the ensuing centuries.

The accusers of Jesus would now see the story go forward on a path leading not to disgrace as they expected but to glory.

CHAPTER 25

At the Cross

The Mother of Jesus and the Beloved Disciple

THE STORY OF THE life of Jesus nears its climax, as does the outline of New Christianity. We have been repeatedly cautioned as we read John's accounts not to take them or any Bible story literally. We have examined the contention that the "sin and salvation" narrative, including the apocryphal "coming again" component, is not at all what John intended. John's narrative deconstructs orthodox Christianity and what millions have been taught about the Bible. In that sense it directly challenges something that has been valuable to many but has also been the root of much harm to many.

We have also seen the gradual unfolding of a new and affirmative way to understand John and indeed to understand Christianity. It represents a gift, especially to those who have been exposed to orthodox Christianity and have left it behind. Again and again, Spong describes Jesus not as the Savior but as the Way, the way to the truth of experiencing a new dimension of humanity, of life. The essence of the Way is love. It is grounded in our oneness with God and with one another, no exceptions. Yes, we hear these terms often. But actually, living them remains a very scary undertaking.

Essential to the challenge to standard Christianity and also essential to some understanding of New Christianity is identifying the point of Jesus' ultimate glory. Standard Christianity locates that point in a physical resurrection, followed by an ascension into heaven from which he will return. Spong sees the high point of Jesus' glory as his crucifixion. It was

PART IV | THE PASSION NARRATIVE

the ultimate expression of love. In the last chapter we saw some of the counterintuitive power that love wields over both organized religion and the state. We saw great strength displayed in what we are conditioned to see as weakness. We saw a mysterious power that does indeed present as a new definition of what it means to be human.

The enigmatic Pilate remains an important introductory player as the crucifixion story continues. Did his encounter with Jesus and the Jewish officials affect him deeply at some level? Did the exchanges represent more than just an ordinary day at work for Rome's representative? Perhaps the treatment of Pilate in the story simply reflects the precarious position of John's authors at the time of the Gospel writing. For whatever reason, Pilate is portrayed here as troubled and uncertain, perhaps understandably troubled about kings and kingdoms.

He orders that a sign reading "Jesus the Nazarene, king of the Jews" be attached to the cross. Given that Jesus is beaten, bloodied, and about to be executed, this might well be seen as simply a gesture of ridicule to discourage his followers.

For the high priests, however, the sign is troubling. Achieving the ignominious death they had been plotting for Jesus was not enough. Perhaps they had reason to be concerned. The universal significance of the life of Jesus is indicated by the fact that the sign was written in Latin, Greek, and Hebrew.

The Jewish officials lobby Pilate to change the wording. In essence they want him to use a word common to media lawyers today: the "alleged" king of the Jews. Even better, the sign should read, "This man said: I am king of the Jews."

Pilate, however, refuses to change the wording. Why? He has already granted the petition calling for the execution. This act could signify the importance to the writers of John of portraying Pilate as at least at the dawn of understanding what Jesus had told him, "Mine is not a kingdom of this world."

Pilate, the symbol of worldly power, makes only one more brief and unenlightening appearance and then disappears from John's story. But perhaps we can still see Pilate in the great earthly powers of today. They go about their business with the same fear, greed, and violence as did Rome. But there is a vague outline of something better tugging at them.

In the story, we are now at another point of departure from standard Christianity. The ultimate glory of Jesus comes when he is "lifted up" on the cross.

John enrobes the details of the crucifixion with messianic Scripture references and quotations. The soldiers inflict a final indignity and take his clothing. But rather than destroy it, the soldiers cast lots for it, as written in Ps 22: "They shared out my clothing among them. They cast lots for my clothes." Pilate makes a brief final appearance when the Jews ask him to have Jesus' legs broken to hasten death so the body would not remain on the cross during the Sabbath. But the soldiers find that he is already dead. Instead, they pierce his side, drawing both water and blood. John cites Scripture passages that bones will not be broken and that witnesses to the event will look upon the one they have pierced.

There is a purpose for this linkage to ancient Scripture. All of the Gospels, as well as the purveyors of official church doctrine, strain mightily to draw a prophetic line from David to Jesus. No one worked harder at that than the writers of Matthew. John does likewise. But, as we shall see, with a very different purpose.

The Messiah is here. Jewish law has been fulfilled, and standard Judaism is no more. There is a new way. The old way is over, but it is not to be cast off. It is to be embraced and reconciled with the new way.

To explain this mystical transformation further, John reintroduces two symbolic characters. The story puts the mother of Jesus and the figure known as "the disciple whom Jesus loved" at the foot of the cross.

The mother of Jesus appears for the first time since the wedding feast at Cana, site of the first sign, the place where Jesus turned the waters of a Jewish purification ritual into wine of the Spirit. Recall, however, that signs themselves only point to meanings they cannot finally enfold. John locates the mother of Jesus at the first sign and at the site of final glorification.

No other Gospel has the mother of Jesus present at his execution. All the magnificent art and literature, the pietas showing her at the foot of the cross were created about nine centuries later. Her appearance here in but one of the four Gospels comes decades after the crucifixion. In short, she was never a major character in the early Christian telling of the Jesus story.

What prompts John to include her? Why is she there, and what role is she to play? She is one symbol of a mystical transition. The other symbolic character is the one described earlier as the "Beloved Disciple" or "the disciple Jesus loved." Recall that he was the one closest to Jesus in the story of the Last Supper. Closer than Peter. He is the only disciple John depicts as following Jesus all the way to the crucifixion.

Again, the Beloved Disciple is not a historical figure but rather a literary creation. The final great creation of the writers of John. Scholars have offered opinions over the years about the identity of this figure. John sees in him a close relation to another symbolic figure, the Lazarus who came back from the dead. Recall that the story of Lazarus was the final sign.

In that story, Mary, sister of Lazarus, contacted Jesus and told him, "Lord, the man you love is ill." Jesus replied that the sickness would not end in the death of Lazarus but "in God's glory, and through it the Son of God will be glorified." In the story of this sign there are several references to the love of Jesus for Lazarus, including the shortest verse in the Bible. When he saw Lazarus, "Jesus wept" for his friend.

Many of the details of the story, including the words of Jesus himself, make it clear to Mary and others that Lazarus is indeed dead. When Mary gently scolds him for not arriving in time to save Lazarus, Jesus tells her that Lazarus will rise again. Mary, perhaps having been schooled in the apocalyptic narrative, says that she is aware that her brother will rise again "at the resurrection on the last day."

Jesus corrects her. Again, using the Jewish name for God, "I AM," he tells Mary, "I am the resurrection (the Way). If anyone believes in me, he will never die." Mary then affirms her belief that Jesus is the Christ.

The story of that sign ends with some Jews coming to believe in Jesus but also with Jewish officialdom beginning its serious plotting against him. Jesus had come to Lazarus at serious personal risk. The Pharisees and high priests had a meeting and decided that Jesus had to die for national security reasons. He might develop a following. Rome might be upset. Who knows what would happen? The words assigned to the high priest Caiaphas indicated a coming struggle over competing visions of what will "unify the scattered children of God." From that day on, official Jewry plotted to kill Jesus.

So ends the story of the final sign. It points to where we are now in the drama. We are at the cross. Jewish powers, otherwise helpless, have sold their spiritual birthright and drawn on their greatest secular power to get their wish.

Present among those close to Jesus are only his mother and her sister, as well as Mary Magdalene and the Beloved Disciple. The other disciples are nowhere to be found. Spong sees the Beloved Disciple as the symbol of those who see, respond, and are transformed. He is the Lazarus who passed from death to life in a process much different than the one envisioned by his sister.

Finally, the "Beloved Disciple" is the symbol of what it means to journey beyond life's defensive boundaries into the mystery of new life, new consciousness, that is to be found in the Christ experience.

The mother of Jesus is the other figure in John's description of a great spiritual transition that took place at the crucifixion. Here, as she did at Cana, she symbolizes Judaism. Recall that in the Cana story she was an integral part of the Jewish ritual that Jesus transformed.

The mother of Jesus stands at the nexus between the shortcomings of the ritual activity of the Jews and the celebration of the new life that Jesus came to bring—new life that is symbolized by the marriage ceremony. The "old wine" has been spent.

Recall that at Cana, she wanted Jesus to solve the wine shortage right away. Jesus was thinking in larger spiritual terms and told her that his time had not yet come. After she told the servants to do whatever Jesus ordered, however, he gave a sign to those gathered at this Jewish wedding feast. From water jars used in Jewish ritual, he provided them with an abundance of something new.

Now at the cross, his time has indeed come. And it was time, through the mother of Jesus and the beloved disciple, to symbolize a transfer from Judaism to a new way.

On the cross, Jesus places his mother, Judaism, in the care of the Beloved Disciple, saying to her, "Woman, this is your son," and to him, "This is your mother." The disciple accepts this responsibility and " . . . made a place for her in his house." This exchange represents a final act of the one of whom the prophets spoke.

It is John's mystical portrait of oneness, of transition to a new consciousness. It should be seen as a profound moment in the Gospel's outline of a New Christianity.

CHAPTER 26

It Is Finished

Water and Blood Flow Together

THE TRANSITION SEEN IN the previous chapter continues, with emphasis on two themes: radical inclusion and continuity with Judaism. Harmonizing the inclusion element of New Christianity with Judaism as it was at the time of Jesus, at the time of the Gospel-writing, and even today, was and is a massive challenge.

Followers of both standard and new Christianity recognize its core teaching: "Love God. Love your neighbor. On these two commandments hang all the Law and the Prophets." In New Christianity everyone is our neighbor. No exceptions. But how do these commandments to love unconditionally relate to "the Law and the Prophets"?

As we have seen, Jesus did not claim to be the only way to love, to a new consciousness of our oneness with God and with one another. But the way that he offered to the world excluded no one. It could not leave out those who did not and would not ever choose to follow it or even those who actively sought to undermine or destroy it. That is the critical contrast between exclusivism and radical inclusion.

Even more than the Samaritan story and the story of the gentile official, the inclusion of the Jews was a difficult and complex component of the door Jesus was opening. In the Jesus story, Jewish officialdom rejected him and plotted his death. At the time John was written, the Christian community included cast-out Jews, gentiles who wanted to be both Christians and practicing Jews, and a growing number of gentiles from across the region. How were they to follow the way, the truth, and the life? How were they to see Judaism?

As the mother of Christianity, Judaism was of special importance to John, the Jewish mystic. The symbolic commitment of Judaism to the care of the Beloved Disciple left no doubt that radical inclusion means everyone. But one key aspect of the path being offered was of particular significance to Judaism. For everyone, Jesus was opening a way to get beyond the innate human tendency to cling to survival and security. He was offering a way to transcend limits. This would prove to be a particularly acute barrier for official Jewry to overcome. It still is.

For Jews in that era, overcoming limits and fears would be especially difficult because of security barriers they had erected in the name of survival as a people. They had been enslaved in Egypt. They had wandered in the wilderness. They had known exile and homelessness. They had codified their security measures in the Torah and other writings they called "the Law." Those measures included a liturgy of ceremony and sacrifice designed to keep them separate from others. They refused to work every seventh day. They would almost never share a meal with someone who was not part of their tribe. They ate a separate diet of foods, separately prepared. They required circumcision as a condition for inclusion. All this they saw as part of a covenant with God. They organized festivals and liturgy around this concept to remind members of it, as well as to pass on their truths through generations.

Now Judaism was being invited to reconsider its security systems. However, it is important to keep in mind John's position that Jesus was not trying to establish a new religion. He offered instead a way to transform the religion of the past by removing its limits, including the limit of isolation.

The truth that this way is the core concept of all-encompassing love, upon which hang all the Law and the Prophets, does not mean that Judaism is denigrated or replaced outright. Rather, John saw Jesus as a new "Word of God," a new Torah spoken to the world.

The "Word of God" in Jesus was destined not to destroy Judaism but to open it to possibilities that were grander and more inclusive than a national life, based on the deep-seated human desire to survive, could ever be or even imagine to be.

All of the Gospel writers saw this need to tell the Jesus story as a continuation of the story of Judaism itself, not a replacement. Accordingly,

John tells the crucifixion story in a way that emphasizes this position. New Christianity sees the crucifixion, not the physical resurrection story, as the ultimate glorification of Jesus. Spong makes several observations to connect that story with Judaism.

In John's Gospel, the crucifixion occurs as the pascal lamb is slaughtered in the Passover ritual. The words attributed to Jesus on the cross, "I thirst" and "it is finished," are linked to Old Testament passages. In this Gospel a soldier pierces Jesus' side with a spear, and water and blood flow out. A passage in Zechariah is "they looked on him whom they had pierced and mourned for him as one mourns for an only son." And, of course, the symbolism evokes the Eucharist and baptism.

This offer of inclusiveness in John's vision of the relationship of Judaism to Christianity is not in itself radially new. It has always been open for anyone to choose a spiritual path or not. The door is open to all, but all do not have to walk through it.

Most Jews, of course, have not. I do not find that disturbing at all. Many paths. One God. (And no one who chooses another path to God or chooses no path is condemned to anything in an afterlife.) What I do find tragic is that the security practice of voluntary non-inclusion can also foster an identity characterized by excessive pride and exclusivism. So it is with many sects today, including Judaism. Many Christians and Jews echo the ancient claim, for example, that Jews are "God's chosen people." This leads to the destructive falsehood that the "Judeo-Christian" tradition is the only way.

For Jews throughout the centuries, there have been good reasons for voluntary isolation. But separation discourages understanding. It also discourages formation of human alliances and support systems. Over time, once Jews were powerless in the sense that the world has come to define power, virulent antisemitism became a relentless reality. There was little understanding or support for Jews.

Even with the dangers of exclusivism, however, isolation has often appeared to be the best survival/security option.

Yet isolation has contributed to unanticipated and catastrophic consequences. Hannah Arendt illustrates some of them in the story of European Jews. She writes that before the advent of nation-states, feudal rulers protected a class of "court Jews" who lent them money to finance wars. Even as nation-states developed, it remained difficult for rulers to raise money for wars by taxing the populace. Consequently, this protected isolation continued until the nineteenth- and early twentieth-century union of capitalism and imperialism. Recall, for example, that the British were only able to acquire the Suez Canal with funding from the Rothschild family. The loan was secured by the full faith and credit of the British Empire.

This lending activity was a perfectly legitimate enterprise. But it provided fodder for lies and distortion and left an isolated community vulnerable when its services were no longer required. I do not profess to understand all of the causes of antisemitism, but I agree with Arendt that isolation was one of them, an unintended consequence.

Imperial businessmen eventually came to provide governments with a new source of funding and caused Jews to lose their exclusive position as state financiers. In the twentieth century, now isolated without protection, Jews were easy targets for hatred, myth, discrimination, and scapegoating. They were unfairly assigned responsibility for many of the sins of capitalism. Ultimately, the German government systematically murdered six million of them. The rest of the world tut-tutted or turned a blind eye and a deaf ear to the Holocaust.

Tragically, instead of highlighting the need to recognize inclusion, human understanding, and oneness, the slaughter had the opposite effect. Jews achieved a homeland in 1948. Their understandable fears after the Holocaust and the damaging exclusivism that is a deadly byproduct of voluntary isolation turned Israel into a brutal state. It is a state now largely isolated from the world community save for one powerful patron. Israel still seeks a security it will not find through isolation and violence.

As noted, in the New Christianity that takes shape in John, it is the crucifixion of Jesus, his victory over death, that opens the door to awareness of the mystical oneness that is the nature of us all. His death was the ultimate revelation of abundant life.

But appreciating that vision depends on a different understanding of an Easter story that is a bedrock of standard Christianity: that Jesus physically arose from the dead three days after the crucifixion, physically went up into heaven, and will physically return, in the words of the Nicene Creed, "to judge both the quick and dead." The final tales of a Jewish mystic offer us that understanding.

PART V

Resurrection
Mystical Oneness Revealed

CHAPTER 27

Introducing John's Story of Easter

THROUGHOUT OUR EXAMINATION OF John, there have been cautions that literalism is the greatest barrier to understanding. Reading the final chapters of this Gospel as the account of a physical resurrection would be an example of such a barrier. Accordingly, it is important to Spong that he conclude the outline of New Christianity by introducing a very different story of Easter. A predicate requirement for understanding that story is to challenge the notion of a physical resurrection and distinguish it from resuscitation. After making that point in this short chapter, he concludes *The Fourth Gospel* with the four final vignettes recounted in John to explain a new and mystical concept of resurrection.

One challenge facing literalists who would characterize the resurrection as a literal physical event is dealing with knowledge we possess today that we did not have two thousand years ago. We now know what would be required.

Physical resurrection would require restarting the heart; reconnecting all arteries, veins, etc.; reversing decay; restoring the gastrointestinal system; and more. In the Jesus story, the skin and skeletal system would also be restored. Jesus would be able to walk as if his feet had not been pinioned to a cross by spikes. Further, he would be able to relate to his friends and others just as if the crucifixion had not happened.

PART V | RESURRECTION

It may be simply argued, of course, that "God can do anything." Most of the world's faith traditions would accept that. But is that what God did here? At least some of the earliest Christian writers may not have been completely sure about that.

There were early Christian writers whose work was not included centuries later in the canon that we read as the Bible. But on this issue, it is important to keep in mind the chronology of writings that were included. Closest to the time of Jesus were the writings of Paul and his supporters, followed by those of the authors of Mark, Matthew, and finally Luke/Acts. It is only in the later writings that physical resurrection first appears, thirty years after the death of Paul.

Paul may be read as arguing for transformation by God. Jesus did not rise; he was raised. He was raised into the life of God, and that life and that process is available to all. Paul writes that mortals must "put on immortality." He speaks of a "spiritual body." Followers of Paul wrote in Colossians: "If then, you have been raised with Christ, seek those things that are above . . . death no longer has dominion over him. The life he lives, he lives to God." Not only had Jesus broken the power of death, God had raised him to a new dimension of life and being. God is the principal actor in Paul's view of the aftermath of the crucifixion. Jesus is a recipient. And all of us are recipients in like manner as well. In the beautifully written Rom 8, Paul writes of Jesus being raised from the dead as a spiritual phenomenon.

Similarly, in 1 Cor 15 he discusses resurrection at length in spiritual rather than physical terms.

It is noteworthy that Mark, the earliest Gospel, has no account of anyone seeing the resurrected Jesus. In that account, Mary of Magdala; Mary, mother of James; and Salome went to the tomb with spices. There, a young man in a white robe told them that the tomb was empty. Jesus was not there. They should go and tell the disciples. The women were frightened and said nothing. Here Mark's Gospel abruptly ends. We will soon see why early Christian writers were later moved to compose a new ending to Mark to comport with the notion of a physical resurrection.

On the resurrection issue, Matthew perhaps advances the literal story, perhaps not. From the vantage point of today's controversy, Matthew might be read as vacillating a bit. The women's visit to the tomb is spiced up by adding an earthquake and changing the man in the white robe to an angel who came down from heaven. Then the writers pick up on the addendum to Mark and have Jesus appear before the women as they are going to inform the disciples. In two short verses, Matthew has Jesus tell the women to go to the disciples and tell them he will see them. That's it.

It is primarily in the later Gospel of Luke that we see the transformation of Jesus into a physical body. By that time many Christians were beginning to get a bit apprehensive because of their understanding that Jesus had promised to return to them soon. Understanding that, one can make an educated guess about the reason for the addendum to Mark and the story in Luke/Acts.

Recall that Paul had written, "Christ, being raised from the dead, will never die again." This presents another problem for literalists. People who rise from the dead, a phenomenon depicted numerous times in Bible stories, eventually must die again. What about Jesus? Only in Luke/Acts do we find an answer asserted—the ascension. So, in this story Jesus does not die again. Rather, the physically resurrected Jesus physically ascends "up there" to be with God. He will come again, to be sure, but he had already told everyone to just be ready and not to speculate on when. That took care of the problem of a resurrected person dying again.

Nevertheless, when Jesus had not returned two or three centuries later, the developing Christian hierarchy somehow established the notion that the "return," for that time at least, had been accomplished in the establishment of the church!

The importance of this component of Christianity for world events should not be underestimated. Professor Bart Ehrman, a highly credentialed biblical scholar, contends that this resurrection story is what sparked the rapid growth of Christianity and its mass appeal to non-Jews even before the "conversion" of the Roman Emperor Constantine. He asserts that without the standard resurrection story, Christianity would have remained a small Jewish cult. He asks us to picture what the world would look like if that had been the case, if some form of the idea that Jesus was God had not become the dominant Western religion, aided immeasurably by approval from the Roman Empire. Ehrman highlights the Easter story, as we have come to understand it, as a defining moment in Western, yea even world history. He may well be correct.

The standard Christian view is not a unanimous one in Christianity. The Unity movement, for example, teaches that Jesus was man becoming God, rather than God becoming man.

John's Gospel appears consistent with this view. It is no surprise that the final chapter presents a very different Easter story. The Fourth Gospel closes by drawing that story from four descriptions of the experience of several characters. In John 20, these accounts appear to flow as a single story. It is Spong's view, however, that each of the four were originally separate parts of early Christian writings but were linked so as to appear to be a continuous narrative. Consequently, he elects to treat each separately. Read that way, each story individually reinforces New Christianity themes we have examined, and each also reveals part of a new vision of resurrection. Through this lens we examine the post-crucifixion experiences first of Mary Magdalene, then of Peter and the Beloved Disciple, followed by that of the other disciples, and finally the disciples again, this time with Thomas present.

CHAPTER 28

Magdalene

Do Not Cling to What Is, Journey into What Can Be

MARY MAGDALENE IS THE principal actor in the first of the stories found in the final chapter of John. We see that only in John is there any substance to this character. Mark just has her standing among those looking at the cross. Later, Matthew simply quotes Mark. Luke also provides no treatise on Mary Magdalene, but there is an interesting twist. Luke briefly identifies her in chapter 8 as one of a group of women who followed Jesus as he went through villages teaching. She was said to be one of a group who had been cured of evil spirits and demons. (In those times spirits and demons could represent virtually any kind of physical or mental abnormality.) John sets out a much fuller story of the role of Mary Magdalene.

Her importance in John's story seems to have presented some worries for those who were putting together the structure of church authority. Several centuries later, Pope Gregory the Great managed to brand her as a prostitute by claiming that she was the woman in the Luke chapter 7 account of Jesus forgiving a woman "who had a bad name in the town." This although the woman was not identified at all in that story.

So, we have the first popular image of Mary Magdalene. We could look on it as just another of the many examples of misogyny perpetrated by the church hierarchy. But here we might also see a reason for the construction of such a negative image—the power of Mary Magdalene among the followers of Jesus. Early writings, and even parts we have seen of the biblical canon that the male leaders approved centuries later, suggest more influence for women in the growth of the early Christian movement than the church fathers were willing to acknowledge.

The founding fathers were probably even more alarmed at another story. Along with other early Christian writings, the events surrounding Mary Magdalene's appearance as the sole mourner at the tomb also furthered speculation that she might have been the wife of Jesus! That speculation is present, for example, in the rock opera *Jesus Christ Superstar*.

Spong does not join that speculation. But he sees John portraying Mary Magdalene as a close associate of Jesus, perhaps as the primary figure in the movement. That is not inconsistent with John's treatment of Mary Magdalene at the empty tomb. She is presented not only to highlight the importance of women, a feature of New Christianity, but also to show us a new and mystical way to see the resurrection.

It is no surprise that we can only understand the post-crucifixion experience of Mary Magdalene as a mystical event if we commit to reading this story other than literally. That caution Spong has repeated again and again. But if we are not to look at what appears to be an account of events that literally happened, what are we to see? How are we to see it?

There is no single answer. It is an intensely individual enterprise for all of us. We have all seen, however, that the minds of each of us can take us to the doorway of a spiritual truth that is itself uniquely ours. Our minds can employ imagination and creativity if we allow that. We have seen in John that signs and symbols are important guides in this effort. Spong advises us to *listen* to the experience it is seeking to open so we can *enter it* and *live into it*. I doubt that many of us are initially adept at reading that way. I certainly was not.

All of which highlights the importance of another helpful means of crossing that mind/spirit threshold—Do not be afraid to look again. That is Mary Magdalene's story. She understood because she "looked again" when she was at the tomb. Her mystical experience reflects the primary motive for this book. Looking again is what I hope those who have been exposed to standard Christianity and rejected it will undertake.

What does it take to be able to look again? Mary came alone, as in truth we all do when we engage in a spiritual experience. She came to the tomb where the remains of a beloved person who had been working to shape her life and her relationship with God were stored. We do not know what impelled her to go. She had arrived before dawn, literally and symbolically.

There was nothing she could have done there other than grieve. Nothing but contemplate the tomb as a terrible symbol of the limits she could see on the meaning of her life and the life of Jesus. Through the literal eyes of the physical world the tomb would be a reminder of those limits. The love of Jesus was finite. His forgiveness was finite. His life was finite. It was all over.

But while still thinking in physical terms, she saw that there was something amiss with this scene of bleak, final despair. The stone had been removed from the entrance of the tomb. Whatever the ultimate explanation for this, it must mean that there was something more to the story. Perhaps the grave had been robbed. Mary's reaction bordered on panic. Then and in the future, how could she quietly honor the life of the man who had taught her so much? She ran to tell Peter and the Beloved Disciple, "They have taken the Lord out of the tomb, and I don't know where they have put him."

They returned to the tomb where Mary collapsed, weeping. Here was a perfectly good place to end Mary Magdalene's part in the story. Now that she had brought the male characters into the narrative, John's account could continue with a glorious story of physical resurrection and ascension. We don't need anything further from her.

But Mary's story does not end. For some unexplained reason, Mary Magdalene looks into the tomb again. She looks again. At that moment her understanding of the mystical begins. It is a process, not an instant jolt of revelation. It parallels the spiritual process that Jesus is experiencing.

We do not know for sure, but perhaps Nicodemus had also looked again. It was he, along with a follower of Jesus named Joseph of Arimathea, who gained permission from Pilate to place the body of Jesus in the tomb that Mary found empty. Nicodemus had brought spices and prepared the body according to Jewish burial customs.

Two angels now appear to Mary and ask why she is weeping. Now somewhere between the physical and mystical, she responds with the same words she spoke to the two disciples. While speaking, again for a reason unexplained, she turns around. Jesus appears and asks the question: "Who are you looking for?" Not yet having made the transition, Mary thinks he is the gardener who may know who took the body and where it has been taken. This fellow could have the answers and give her a chance to retrieve the body. She could continue on the physical level of grief, respect, and regret that had likely moved her to go to the tomb.

But then her decision to look again bore fruit. She heard Jesus say "Mary!" and "She knew him." She answered "Rabbuni!" a term of high respect reserved for use by one who was a devoted pupil of a revered teacher, or by the wife of such a figure.

Jesus told her not to cling to him because he was in the process of ascending to the Father and God of them both. He was escaping human limits. He told her to find the disciples. She did so and said to them, "I have seen the Lord," words with far more mystical than physical significance.

The Synoptic Gospel depictions of what can be seen as physical resurrection and ascension occurred forty days later than what is set out in the story we are following here. Another small reminder about literalism.

What Mary was finally able to understand mystically differed greatly from the despairing finality that struck her physical senses at the tomb. Death now has not separated her from living the abundant loving life to which Jesus had shown her the way. She has entered into a new mystical awareness. She and others have the rest of their earthly lives to live. No barrier, no limit can endure if they walk through the doorway of love that Jesus had opened. He had revealed that life and consciousness are very different if we can achieve the freedom that he did: to go beyond the drive to survive and instead be the love God is. Once barriers are down, the door is opened to mystical oneness with God and with all others.

Spong closes the first of the four resurrection stories this way: *John is painting an interior experience in external colors using objective words. What Mary Magdalene saw when she said, "I have seen the Lord" was the meaning of life. She steps into it and claims it for her own. That is how Easter always dawns.*

What of Peter and the Beloved Disciple to whom Mary went upon discovering that the tomb had been disturbed? Can a standalone story of their experience tell us more about a mystical take on resurrection?

CHAPTER 29

Peter and the Beloved Disciple

Resurrection Dawns Without a Body

THIS VIGNETTE MAY REMIND some of us of "compare and contrast" examination questions. Here, John engages in that exercise using the historical character of Peter and the literary symbol we have seen called the Beloved Disciple.

In the process of understanding the mystical significance of the physical, the Beloved Disciple is always ahead of Peter, just as he has always been closer to Jesus in the stories we have seen.

When Mary tells them of the empty tomb, the two go to see for themselves. The Beloved Disciple arrives first. There is no body. Jesus has already transcended the limits of death. He has been raised to a new dimension of life. But what both disciples do see are the burial cloths on the ground and the cloth that covered the face of Jesus rolled up in a place by itself.

Reminding us that mystical understanding is a process rather than an instant experience, John writes that neither disciple yet had a full understanding of the resurrection. Yet only the Beloved Disciple is said at that moment to have "believed." On the same evidence, and without assistance from apparitions, one of the disciples comes sooner to a mystical understanding of physical signs. Peter struggles to see meaning beyond the limits that life imposes.

That is not to say that because Peter struggled while his fellow follower understood; Peter never got it. The story only serves to remind us that in every endeavor, temporal or spiritual, someone will always be ahead of us. We should be thankful for understanding that.

Peter and the Beloved Disciple appear again only in an appendix to the Gospel, probably written later by another follower. Spong does not choose to write of it. Here, Jesus appears to all the disciples. It may be noteworthy that while he is telling Peter to "feed my sheep," Peter turns to see the Beloved Disciple following them. Perhaps Peter's struggle has now borne fruit? Jesus has just told him that he would die the death of a martyr. Perhaps Peter has come to understand that death will have no dominion over him.

CHAPTER 30

Pentecost

The Second Coming of Jesus— It Was "A Little While"

How did this very different resurrection story we are following blend with John's vision of how the Jesus story developed and grew from Judaism? Why does that matter? Because this connection is essential to recognizing the new and radical narrative that John presents. A narrative that tells a different Jesus story and reveals a New Christianity.

The writers of John were aware of heroic figures in the story of Judaism who had experienced oneness with God at the end of their human lives in a manner that did not require death and resuscitation. It was important to tell the resurrection story in a way that would help new Jewish Christians understand the connection to Hebrew Scriptures, including these well-known figures.

In Jewish lore, the earliest of these stories involved Enoch, a righteous early descendant of Adam. Enoch walked with God, but then "he vanished because God took him." The stories of Moses and Elijah may be more familiar to Christians today because of their prominence in the other three Gospels. At the time of his death, Moses was reported to be in direct conversation with God. It was God who is said to have buried him, but no grave was ever found. The death of Elijah, "father of the prophetic movement," was even more dramatic. A chariot of fire appeared, and he was swept up in a whirlwind.

Typical of the importance of Moses and Elijah in the Synoptics is the story found in Luke. Jesus took Peter, James, and John with him to a mountain to pray. The three see Moses and Elijah appear. They are talking with Jesus about his passing. They "saw his glory."

Awed but elated, Peter suggests building tents for Jesus, for Moses, and for Elijah. But the disciples are in for a more important experience. As Peter speaks, a cloud descends, and a voice confirms that Jesus is the chosen one and urges them to listen to him. The connection is made and reinforced.

In none of these stories, including all related to the death of Jesus, is a physically resurrected body discovered. Indeed, the idea of such a physical event would have been foreign to John, the Jewish mystic. What occurred at the moment of oneness with God is perceived as a mystical experience, not a physical event. As parts of the vine, that oneness is open to us all. If the life of the vine flowed through the branches, the oneness of life itself was held in common.

There was another distinction between John's mystical vision of the resurrection and what would come to be the standard Christian narrative. As we have seen, the standard Easter story also depended on the "second coming of Jesus" in a way that John's vision certainly did not. The Nicene Creed, constructed centuries later, reminds millions of Christians today that Jesus "ascended into heaven, from whence he shall come again to judge both the quick and the dead."

But when? We have looked at Paul's attempt after some fifty years had passed to reassure Christians that the "dead in Christ" would be taken care of when Jesus returned. How would John's new Christians feel when ninety years or so had passed since the promise? Was the now deeply embedded second coming expectation a mistake, or had the Jesus story been misunderstood all along?

John chooses the latter and so undertakes to reinterpret this foundational tenet. With the Jewish hero stories in mind as context, Spong asserts that the Lazarus story we examined in chapter 16 was part of the new Easter narrative. Recall that in that account Jesus did not respond to the entreaties of Mary and Martha until Lazarus was well and truly dead. In fact, the women rebuked him for the delay. After correcting the disciples and pronouncing that Lazarus was in fact dead, Jesus said, "I am glad I was not here so that you may believe."

There we have for purpose of contrast what can easily be seen as a physical resuscitation story. There is a corpse. Lazarus has clearly been dead for several days.

So how to compare with the Jewish stories of figures who did not undergo death and physical resurrection? How to understand the story of Mary Magdalene who came to see that she could not cling to the physical presence of Jesus? And how to understand the story of Peter and the Beloved Disciple, where one of them saw on the bare evidence in the tomb that Jesus had already transcended the limits of death? How to understand all of these are stories where there was no corpse?

The unconnected stories of Mary Magdalene and the two disciples at the tomb each tell us of a different aspect of the new interpretation of the resurrection and the second coming. John adds another critical component in the story of Jesus appearing to the disciples on the evening of the same day as the first two stories.

This story is also clearly not about a physical resurrection. The disciples have locked the doors of a room for fear of those whose mission to kill Jesus had been successful. Jesus enters through the locked doors. To remove any doubt of his identity in what must have been a startling appearance, he pronounces, "Peace be upon you" and shows them his pierced hands and side.

For some reason, standard Christianity has paid a great deal of attention to these acts. But they remind me of my many meetings with FBI agents who came to my office when one of my students had applied for a security clearance. The first act of these agents was to produce their credentials. But the substance of our meeting was certainly not about who they were.

So it was with the vision of Jesus appearing before the disciples. There had been many exchanges about who he was, but the substance of this meeting was Pentecost. As God had done with Adam in Hebrew mythology, Jesus breathed on the disciples, saying, "Receive the Holy Spirit." This was the empowering and commissioning of the disciples, and it was about life. The community was to be the source of life, and its members could offer a new more abundant life to all who could learn to overcome security measures and be free to give their lives away in love, as he had done.

The second coming was not to be a measurable external event. The second coming is the birth of all those who choose the light and enter into the mystical source of oneness with God.

PART V | RESURRECTION

In John's view, the spirit that Jesus brought into the world and gave to all showed the way to a new dimension of life in which loving enough will overcome the ability of the world to distort, hurt, and kill.

So it is with the outline of a New Christianity. Spong sees the resurrection as something that can occur in each of us, not a physical event in the life of Jesus. *The Christian life is not about believing creeds and being obedient to divine rules; it is about living, loving, and being. Resurrection comes when we are free to give our lives away . . .*

He says of the second coming: *He could open the door for us all to step into the reality of God. The glorification of Jesus was in the crucifixion; the return of Jesus was in the impartation of the spirit on Easter evening. From Friday to Sunday is in fact "a little while." There is to be no further wait for the second coming.*

The last of the four vignettes addresses both this Jesus story and a component of the early Christian congregation. It is about the famous "doubting Thomas."

CHAPTER 31

Thomas

The Final Witness, the Ultimate Claim

JOHN GIVES THOMAS CONTENT and prominence in the Easter story. The earlier Gospels did no more than list him among the disciples.

Some Christians, however, know also of the Gospel of Thomas, a short collection of sayings attributed to Jesus. There was a great debate among scholars when its full text was discovered in 1945. Some even wanted to make Thomas the fifth official Gospel. This is simply another reminder that two hundred to three hundred years after the time about which John writes, members of the Christian hierarchy picked and chose among documents for inclusion in the official canon. In the end, Thomas did not make the cut.

John, however, makes Thomas an important figure at two points. First, recall that in the powerful meeting with the disciples known as the farewell discourses, Jesus tells them that they know the way he is to travel.

Thomas, still thinking literally, does not yet understand and speaks up: "Lord, we do not know where you are going, so how can we know the way?" With this question, Thomas triggers a reply from Jesus that becomes perhaps the verse most misunderstood by members of today's standard Christian community, especially evangelicals. But as we have seen, the reply is also a mystical key to a new understanding of the Jesus story. As we have also noted in the examination of the story of the man born blind at birth, Jesus is speaking of himself as the shower of a way to a new consciousness, a new awareness of oneness with God and all others: "You will understand that I am in my Father and you in me and I in you." Jesus trying to explain a "way" that Thomas does not yet understand. Philip is shown to be in the same place. Curiously, he also seems to preview the later role of Thomas in the resurrection story. Philip asks, "Lord, let us see the Father, and then we shall be satisfied."

Jesus patiently explains what the disciples can do for the world when they come to understand the way. He tells them that they will perform even greater works than he.

Later, as John's Easter story concludes, Thomas appears again. It is a second story of Jesus appearing through locked doors to speak with the disciples. We learn that Thomas was not present at the first meeting. He is, however, the central figure in this one.

Perhaps remembering from the earlier exchange that Thomas does not yet understand the way, Jesus invites Thomas to put his hand in his wounded side: "Doubt no longer but believe." What follows is often not a part of the popular understanding of "doubting Thomas." For Thomas does not accept Jesus' invitation to rely on worldly evidence. He does not put his hand in Jesus' side. Instead, he simply replies, "My Lord and my God." Like Peter, Thomas is gradually moving from dark to light. He is coming to understand that when we see Jesus, we see God. Thomas is no longer dependent on physical evidence. He is coming to see the way in terms of mystical oneness, not geography.

Jesus reminds him of the blessings and the abundant life there for all those who will understand even without seeing him. Understanding the way and offering it will be the Pentecost mission of the disciples. In that mission, the disciples will be recognized by the love they give and the freedom to give their lives away in love to others, as Jesus did.

The concluding paragraph of John's Gospel points again to the purpose of Jesus. He came and taught about life. This human experience. Now. It asserts that there are many other signs that Jesus worked that are not recorded in the Gospel. That the ones we have examined were recorded "so that you may believe that Jesus is the Christ, the son of God, and that believing this, you may have life through his name." *To have life—not to become religious . . . but to have life . . . the experience of living in which we . . . cross the boundaries of fear that separate us from one another and from ourselves.*

Thus concludes John's Gospel. Its message was for the skeptics in John's community as well as for skeptics today. Jesus did not come down from heaven, and he has not physically returned from there. But contrary to what a friend's uncle once told me (really), Russian cosmonaut Yuri Gagarin was not the antichrist, and Armageddon is not just around the corner. What has been somewhat pretentiously termed "apocalyptic eschatology" is not a component of New Christianity.

For me, "I don't know" is always an acceptable answer. The entire New Testament can certainly be read to support the standard sin and salvation narrative as an extension of a perception of the divine that is reflected in standard Judaism. It is a narrative that could be true. It has been a blessing to some and caused much harm to others. But John the Jewish mystic tells another Jesus story. It is a story that has been hidden for too long.

CHAPTER 32

The Epilogue

Resurrection Is Not Physical, but It Is Real

SOMETIME AFTER THE GOSPEL was written, some in John's community added a brief epilogue. It must be included in the Easter story because it recounts yet another post-crucifixion appearance of Jesus to some of the disciples.

The epilogue is significant for Spong. I see it as less important, and it presents another challenge to presenting this outline of New Christianity in simple, non-scholarly terms. But after all, we are describing the work of an eminent biblical scholar who is arguing for a non-literal, mystical understanding of the basic elements of Christianity.

For virtually all of the book so far, Spong has presented this argument in a way that is consistent with my training as a lawyer. He has offered evidence in support of his conclusions, although the conclusions take us beyond the realm of evidence and reason. The strength and resonance of the evidence can be evaluated by the reader. In this final chapter, the good bishop sets out scholarly matters that may seem trivial to lay people such as we. The final piece of evidence he asks us to accept is simply his lifetime of work, particularly on a new understanding of the resurrection. He then concludes the book with quite eloquent summary statements about the resurrection and New Christianity itself. I believe we should forgive Spong the generalizations that are not specifically supported by evidence in the epilogue and consider that lifetime of work. In my view, he is simply

THE EPILOGUE

summarizing his brilliant gift of a new way to make the Jesus story a valuable force in our lives and in the world.

The setting of the epilogue is clearly sometime after the crucifixion. Perhaps weeks, perhaps longer. Seven of the disciples, including Peter and the Beloved Disciple, are trying to get beyond their grief and return to normal life. Peter has returned to fishing.

Jesus appears and calls out to them. The Beloved Disciple is the first to recognize him. They have not been successful to that point, but Jesus shows them how to fill the nets abundantly with fish. He then suggests that they have a meal together. Afterward, Jesus takes Peter aside. He commissions Peter to "feed my lambs . . . look after my sheep." He also advises that Peter will die the death of a martyr.

This exchange marks the first time Peter takes precedence over the Beloved Disciple. This is emphasized as the story continues. The Beloved Disciple is walking behind Jesus and Peter. The two discuss stories then circulating about the Beloved Disciple, but it is clear that the mantle of leadership is now to be worn by Peter.

The epilogue concludes with the writer, who claims to be one of the disciples, vouching for its truth and reminding us that all of the works of Jesus are far too numerous to be recorded.

The story, of course, is almost identical to the one set out in Luke. There, Jesus came upon Peter and his partners James and John. The only difference is that Luke's story was not about resurrection. Rather, it could be seen as a foretelling of the epilogue's commissioning story. In Luke, Jesus told the disciples he would have them draw in people, not fish.

Spong undertakes an explanation of why the epilogue was written and what it means. Some of the more scholarly observations that I have mentioned but will not detail here reinforce his conclusion that this story had to have been set a significant amount of time after the crucifixion. One of the factors cautioning us again that we are not to take the story literally is the use of Peter, a historical figure, alongside the Beloved Disciple, a literary creation.

Other than being yet another story of Jesus appearing to people after the crucifixion, what does the story have to do with the resurrection? We come to the point of relying on Spong's lifetime of work on that subject to see the connection:

PART V | RESURRECTION

> *I am convinced that this chapter, though not an essential part of the Fourth Gospel, is based on a very early primitive record that may reflect a tradition even earlier than the gospel resurrection stories.*

If Spong is correct, we can learn how the meaning of Jesus dawned on the disciples, a dawning that did not involve marveling at a physical resuscitation.

He then reprises the evidence from the four vignettes against a physical resurrection, before asserting that the experience of the resurrection was nevertheless real: *while the resurrection is not physical, it is not nothing.*

He goes on to explain that the spiritual dawning occurred in Galilee not Jerusalem, that Peter was the central figure in the experience, that three months to a year elapsed before the full awakening of consciousness that Jesus was of God and death could not contain him.

Finally, the meaning of resurrection was made known through the breaking of bread. Spong recalls the many instances of this recounted in all the Gospels, from the multiple accounts of feeding multitudes, the Last Supper and, of course, the meal shared in the epilogue.

This dawning of consciousness, the resurrection, was an inner experience of transformation that broke all human limits and achieved union with that which we call God. Spong sees it most clearly set out in the epilogue. By understanding the life that Jesus gave away in love, the disciples led by Peter could learn that perfect love is giving one's life away for others:

> *One cannot know the essence of love until one can love another—not because another deserves love but because another simply is. One cannot be all that one can be unless one frees others to be all that they can be. This is what Jesus means. This is what resurrection is. This is what the cross means. This is what life in the spirit is all about.*

I repeat here Spong's hope for his legacy, found in the final words of *The Fourth Gospel*: *This also becomes for me the basis upon which we can build "A New Christianity for a New World." To that task Christianity is now called.* I share that hope.

Afterword

As this work progressed, I became increasingly aware that some of the challenges to getting beyond reason are reflected in the limits of the languages we have available for communication with one another. We have, for example, become inured to terms such as "love" and "oneness." We have heard them too many times. We are almost incapable of understanding and relating those words to our daily lives. What could it possibly mean to be "one with God and one with all others"? Yet that is the "Way" set out in John's mystical Jesus story. And what about "unconditional love"? In other writings, Spong uses a powerful phrase. He claims that Jesus urges us to "love wastefully." I see that as an invitation not to be concerned about limits on whom we love, or how much, or for how long.

Yet how much help does standard Christianity offer its members in probing the more difficult challenges to making these terms meaningful? Do creeds and literal Bible reading provide anything? And what of those who have been exposed to organized religion and walked away? What of those who have never bothered with spiritual matters at all? These groups represent the majority of Western society. Does the state of that society today offer any serious means of examining these terms?

These are all limits to having life and having it abundantly. But the Jesus story in New Christianity is about overcoming limits. Individual limits that prevent us from even grappling with the idea of a relationship with what, by many names, is called God.

I have acknowledged that anything having to do with taking that on is an intensely individual matter. Perhaps there is nothing as close to unique for each of us. Nevertheless, I hope that a summary of my own spiritual experience to date may offer you some encouragement in making the effort to overcome limits. My story may have similarities to that of many who have tried and eventually rejected standard Christianity. My story will not be identical, but I believe that many of you may recognize some common stops on our respective journeys. If so, I hope that it will embolden you to give that big question some serious consideration.

I am a disciple of Bishop John Shelby Spong. I do not see every issue as he does. I wish he was still with us so I could ask him about several matters. However, not only does the New Christianity resonate with me; I am grateful that it gave me a spiritual place to go. For several years, disenchanted with standard Christianity, I explored different paths. From that exploration I learned much of value. But like Spong, ultimately, I knew I had to follow the only path I knew. If possible. Spong's vision of a new and different Christian path opened up that possibility for me. I believe it might do that also for some of you.

HIGHLAND PARK BAPTIST CHURCH

My exposure to different paths and to offshoots of the same path has been a blessing. It began in the fundamentalist Highland Park Baptist Church (HPB) in 1940s Chattanooga, Tennessee. This was a remarkable institution. Long before the rise of megachurches, long before televangelists, long before most people even had TV, HPB services saw four thousand people in attendance along with a hundred-voice choir and a forty-piece orchestra. The church later established Tennessee Temple College. As a law professor, I had the honour of teaching one of its graduates.

Highland Park Baptist stuck strictly to the basic sin, sacrifice, and salvation narrative. About sin, very strictly. No playing cards. No going to movies or Chattanooga Lookouts baseball games on Sunday, for example.

The weekly schedule was pretty full. Sunday School, morning and evening church services. (Driving home from Sunday evening service, you could listen to a radio program broadcast from the church chapel.) Wednesday night prayer meeting. Thursday night visitation. (I would go with my grandfather to visit those who had been absent from Sunday School and tell them how much we missed them.)

Yes, it was decidedly what we term today a fundamentalist evangelical church. But my experience there gave me at least three blessings, the value of which I am still coming to appreciate.

First, from Sunday School, I was taught that "God is love." In later years, I have come to some understanding of this powerful mystery. This statement expresses what is at the same time the simplest and most complex concept known to humankind.

Second, and important to the first, HPB differed from many fundamentalist evangelical churches today in an important respect. It never tried to tell us who our enemies were supposed to be. I was raised never being taught to associate God with hostility towards those who were different. I am grateful for that.

Third, my experience gave me a solid grounding in Bible study—at least the King James version. I participated in "Sword Drills," based on a comment by Paul in Ephesians that the word of God was a sword. The exercises resembled a spelling bee. What I learned not only taught me the importance of the Bible to Christianity; it also gave me in later years a valuable research tool. In law, for example, if you can remember a well-known case on a subject, that will lead you quickly to relevant material on more precise matters in its area. So it is with the Bible, and "sword drill" got me started.

CERTIFIED EPISCOPALIAN

In my university years, I became more and more troubled by the sin and salvation narrative. HPB had taught a real heaven "up there" and a real hell "down there." Who went where was determined by who had accepted Jesus as their personal savior. (Once that was done, it was irrevocable. You could "backslide," but you were permanently "saved" and could never again be bound for hell, no matter what you did.) Even if the approach to the "lost" was not to attack them but to save them, this just did not resonate.

At age 20, I literally looked in a mirror and said, "You don't believe this stuff."

Episcopalians embraced essentially the same narrative but seemed to smooth its hard edges. Importantly, they were tolerant of questioning. At every ritual (like every political campaign event), there is a choice of what to emphasize and what to omit or downplay. Episcopalians don't do fire and brimstone.

They were also pretty tolerant. I learned this when my wife and I became tenants in the campus Canterbury House. In lieu of rent, my responsibility was to keep the coal furnace stoked and serve as acolyte at every service. The latter task gave me an appreciation of ritual and symbolism that continues to this day.

Eventually, I decided to convert formally. It was in a required nine-week "Enquirers Class" that I shocked the teachers a bit. Episcopalians and Roman Catholics claim for their bishops an apostolic succession, going one person after another from St. Peter right down to the current prelate. I had just completed a course in Tudor and Stuart England in which I had done quite well. It seemed to me that apostolic succession was something of a problem, especially for Episcopalians and Anglicans. I told the church instructor that I knew theirs was really just a branch of Henry VIII's church, but that was OK. I still wanted to join.

In spite of this glitch, they made me a certified Episcopalian. It was a label I would wear, at least formally, until I was 60. There were times when that was significant. For example, it was from an Episcopalian organization that I was led to become North Carolina's chief attorney for migrant farmworkers. That experience included working side-by-side in hostile territory with members of the social justice branch of the Roman Catholics, people I will always admire. No one who witnessed the intentional degradation of human beings such as that visited upon farmworkers in a land of plenty could escape thinking of its spiritual dimensions—and once again questioning the standard Christian narrative.

UNITY MOVEMENT

Here I experienced defining moments that not only made past events understandable but also opened the way to thoughtful consideration of Spong's New Christianity. These two lanes on the Christian path are beautifully similar.

The Unity Movement (not Unitarians) was founded in the late nineteenth century by Charles and Myrtle Fillmore. Today there are Unity congregations of various sizes around the world. I have joined with a congregation numbering five while teaching in Tuscaloosa, Alabama, and with hundreds while visiting my sister in Tucson, Arizona, and my sister-in-law in Chevy Chase, Maryland.

Discovering Unity was a valuable experience in itself. In 2000 my wife and I had moved to Canada. In many years of fighting the death penalty, we had seen and experienced the brutal underside of the United States justice

AFTERWORD

system. We had also noticed some of the many signs of fascism that would become the clear and present danger that exists there today.

We joined a congregation of Anglicans, the Canadian version of Episcopalians. It was a very progressive parish, concerned about social justice and focused on the teachings of the Gospels about love. Unfortunately, the parish was part of a diocese that, then and now, is operated as a business, not a ministry. I have no doubt that this has helped me understand Spong's antipathy toward religious hierarchies, Jewish and Christian.

The path from this happy place to Unity was influenced by my relationship with the parish priest. A former Roman Catholic, he had come to us from Colombia. His English was not great. I read the Eucharist rite into a tape recorder for him, which treated the congregation to hearing a Colombian with a Virginia accent!

The priest took seriously the Gospel teachings about the least of us. He slept on the sidewalks with the homeless. He sheltered many of them in the church during winter.

One day he came to me and said: "Beel! I have found three hundred breads!" That was the beginning of the Rainbow Kitchen, which continues to this day. Now operated by a parish of the United Church of Canada, the rules are still the same. No rules. Anyone who comes in is fed a full meal, and thousands have come over the years. I think I have a special understanding of the loaves and fishes story.

I became warden and was quite active in the church. In 2005, the priest told me that there was a group called Unity of Victoria that gave money each month to a local charity. They had selected Rainbow Kitchen, and he sent me to accept a check at a little ceremony that was part of their Sunday service.

At the service, I noticed a sign reading, "We invite and welcome all people, of all faiths. We express universal principles of love, truth and oneness with God as a way of life." I was to learn how powerful those words are. Also, two rows ahead of me as I waited to receive the Unity donation was a lesbian couple. I knew then that the welcoming sign was serious. I resolved to come back and explore further.

At the time, I had just about had it with Anglicans and Episcopalians tying themselves in theological knots over whether two misconstrued verses in Romans meant that gays and lesbians could be excluded from full acceptance into the church. At one point, I attended a full "smells and bells" service at the grand cathedral in Victoria where Queen Elizabeth II worshiped when she visited. The service was followed by a discussion of whether this writing of St. Paul was "credal," i.e., gave authority to exclude LGBT+ people. In a later Canada-wide meeting, where majority votes of bishops, lay delegates, and priests were required, only the vote of the bishops determined that it was. So, no inclusion. The hand-wringing continues to this day, no doubt further explaining my view and Spong's about authority and hierarchy.

Not long thereafter, the powers that be in the diocese happily took the opportunity to make our parish the first of ten to be shut down. They had been consolidating and closing parishes for some time. Our social justice activism had not been well received, so it must have been good news when they learned that our priest had succumbed to one of the diverse failures of humankind. He had an affair with a congregant.

The closing left my wife and me with no church home. She was a lifelong Episcopalian and eventually found another relatively progressive Anglican parish. I began involvement with Unity of Victoria.

I was then called out of retirement to return for a year to teach at Washington and Lee Law School, where I had spent more than twenty years. I had been a member of Robert E. Lee Memorial Episcopal Church. My first inquiry on arrival was about R. E. Lee's position on full participation for gays and lesbians. Unfortunately, the church was also immersed in exclusionary theological nonsense. I was still without a church.

Eventually, a colleague told me that there was a large Unity congregation in Roanoke, some fifty-five miles away. For the rest of the year, I made that trip, and it was a spiritually enriching experience. Unity of the Roanoke Valley is where I learned that God is "in here," not "up there."

On return to Canada, I became active in Unity of Victoria. Here I came to accept a vision of my relation to God that was starkly different from the prevailing Christian narrative but completely compatible with the basic truth I had learned so long ago at HPB: God is love.

A host of powerful implications of that phrase unfolded for me during the years I spent with Unity. All of them may be found in the New Christianity I have outlined here. They include:

No exclusivism. No "chosen people." A sign outside the Unity offices read: "Many paths. One God." Honor every faith tradition. Remember that Christians are a distinct global minority.

No dogma. No doctrine. As that sign on my first visit read, "We express universal principles . . ." We do not dictate or authoritatively pronounce. No

AFTERWORD

requirements to be a part of the movement. Complete freedom to discuss and challenge any aspect. No theological hierarchy.

Another highly significant phrase in the sign that first caught my eye: "... oneness with God as a way of life." If God is love, then so am I. That is true for everyone, so we are one with one another. That unity is expressed in the two New Testament commandments and in the versions of the golden rule that are found in every major faith tradition.

Which leads to the next principle: we are all spirits having a human experience. If we are one with God, and God is love, then God is a spirit of love. I came to visualize a Great Spirit of Love, with a love for me and for everyone that is unconditional, infinite, and eternal. Each of these aspects is mind-boggling. A spirit of a love that cannot be earned and cannot be lost. Love with no quantitative limit and no expiration date. The kind of love the tales of the Jewish mystic described.

This unlimited love also rests within me. In that sense, I am God. The limiting difference lies in my *awareness*, in my *inhibited consciousness* of my own divinity. The same is true of everyone. In trying to grasp the implication of this, I find a definite affinity with the message and the mysticism that Spong saw in John's gospel. It is not about sin, salvation, and the afterlife. It is about how to live life more abundantly as spirits on a human journey. Today. It is about our spirits drawing wisdom and guidance. It is about love from the Great Spirit of Love increasing our consciousness. It is about going beyond reason. It is about overcoming limits.

What about this Jesus person? I found that my Unity brothers and sisters had some trouble with this. Perceptions differ. But Unity also sees Jesus as a Way-Shower and a master teacher. On that there is agreement.

This is also a vision that by no means excludes the possibility of other Way-Showers and master teachers at other times in history and as a part of other faith traditions. One, for example, could be Bahaullah, founder of the Baha'i faith tradition. In the teachings of this nineteenth-century prophet, you will find nothing inconsistent, and much in common with the Jesus story as Spong and I see it. You just have to get over the strange sounding names and accept the possibility that God did not end revelations to humans two thousand years ago.

My brothers and sisters in Unity Victoria were and are among the finest people I have ever known. They are simply a joy to be around.

My only serious concern was that Unity focused too much on inner peace and not nearly enough on advancing world peace. Unity endorses something called the "ripple effect." It holds that if we as individuals live peacefully and lovingly, that will spread like ripples in a pond eventually bring peace to the world. I had trouble with that. I still do. I had resigned my commission in the army and committed my life to nonviolence in 1969. The war on Vietnam was a defining event in my life, and ripples did not seem nearly enough.

By the time of my experience in Unity, I had long since returned to the peace activism in which I had engaged earlier. By now I clearly understood what I had not before. Peace action for me had to be intertwined with my spiritual experience. Over the years, I had certainly witnessed compassionate action by people who would never be part of a faith community. But for me, it had to be all of one cloth. Oneness with all either was or it wasn't. If it was, antiwar actions from faith communities were sorely needed. I admit that at times I was quite unhelpfully intemperate about this.

In particular, Canada's subservience to the United States war-makers had always bothered me. When Unity Victoria refused to be part of a message from religious leaders simply asking the government to abandon joint planning for an invasion of Venezuela, I got angry and left. I probably should not have done that.

SPIRITUAL WANDERING

I had learned a lot. And it all fit. HPB Sunday School had taught me the most basic truth: God is love. Episcopalians and Anglicans taught me how that played out in real life matters of social justice—and some of the challenges involved in trying to live life without distinguishing between secular and spiritual. Unity taught me about radical inclusion and oneness, about my own inner divinity.

I began searching. I was searching for a place to gather with others regularly, searching for some semblance of a church.

I joined my wife's Anglican church for awhile, and it was a wonderful experience until the priest was reassigned. Under her leadership, the focus had always been to address every issue in light of the New Testament commandments. If doctrine ever got in the way of that, we just ignored doctrine. When it became apparent that the next priest talked a good game but basically ran a standard timid parish, I was on the road again.

I connected with a congregation called the Victoria Truth Centre. The centre is part of a spiritual movement called "New Thought." I share much of the movement's vision of God as a divine presence. But New Thought seemed to ignore the Jesus story altogether.

Unity Victoria has frequently given me the honor of being the speaker at Sunday service. After I left Unity, it also came to pass for a time that I spoke at Truth Centre services every other month.

Even though I came to conclude that this was not the congregation I had been searching for, I cherished my time with the splendid people at the centre.

(I was honored recently to be invited back to facilitate a workshop on the relationship of Spong's work to New Thought and Unity.)

The intense research, thought, and prayer required of a lay person preparing to speak publicly about spiritual matters over the years has focused my mind on further development of that bedrock HPB truth—God is love.

I have begun to speak about the practical implications of that simple statement. If we were spirits having a human journey, perhaps the Great Spirit of Love had attributes that could guide us on that journey. They include compassion, understanding, patience, forgiveness, and many more. That concept in fact was perhaps St. Paul's greatest gift to us when he wrote:

> Love is always patient and kind; it is never jealous; love is never boastful or conceited; it is never rude or selfish; it doesn't take offence, and is not resentful. Love takes no pleasure in other people's sins but delights in the truth; it is always ready to excuse, to trust, to hope, and to endure whatever comes.

ACTIVE CONTENTMENT

As did Bishop John Shelby Spong, I have come to a place of contentment in my later years. I am still learning and growing. But I don't need a place to do this. My Unity community now meets once a month. I join them. I am occasionally the speaker. I offer some aspects of the new Jesus story. It is enough.

I share this view expressed once by John Spong: *I am content to learn from those who follow a different path and walk side-by-side with them toward a God who, I believe, is beyond the images that bind and blind us all.*

Honoring and learning from other paths, Spong nevertheless felt that he had to follow the only one he knew but with a very different vision. So do I. That is the reason I have tried here to resurrect his New Christianity.

PART V | RESURRECTION

Using *The Fourth Gospel*, I have tried to free the New Christianity from its paternalistic pigeonhole placement in the dusty archives of theology and highlight its life value to a diverse audience. New Christianity was a gift to me. A gift that should be resurrected and shared.

Bibliography

Arendt, Hannah. *The Origins of Totalitarianism*. New York: Houghton Mifflin Harcourt 1968.
Armstrong, Karen. *The Bible: A Biography*. Vancouver: Douglas and McIntyre, 2007.
———. *Fields of Blood: Religion and the History of Violence*. Toronto: Knopf Canada, 2014.
———. *In the Beginning*. Toronto: Random House, 1996.
Borg, Marcus J. *Reading the Bible Again for the First Time*. New York: Harper Collins, 2001.
Brakke, David. "Understanding the New Testament." https://www.thegreatcourses.com/courses/understanding-the-new-testament.
Ehrman, Bart. "How Jesus Became God." https://www.thegreatcourses.com/courses/how-jesus-became-god.
Levine, Amy-Jill. "Great Figures of the New Testament." https://www.thegreatcourses.com/courses/great-figures-of-the-new-testament.
Macy, Joanna, and Chris Johnstone. *Active Hope: How to Face the Mess We're in Without Going Crazy*. Novato, CA: New World Library, 2012.
Spong, John Shelby. *Here I Stand*. New York: Harper Collins, 2001.
———. *Jesus for the Non-Religious*. New York: Harper Collins, 2007.
———. *The Fourth Gospel: Tales of a Jewish Mystic*. New York: Harper Collins, 2013.